Every school a
great school

Every school a great school

Realizing the potential of system leadership

David Hopkins

Open University Press

Open University Press
McGraw-Hill Education
McGraw-Hill House
Shoppenhangers Road
Maidenhead
Berkshire
England
SL6 2QL

email: enquiries@openup.co.uk
world wide web: www.openup.co.uk

and Two Penn Plaza, New York, NY 10121-2289, USA

First published 2007

Reprinted 2008, 2009

A catalogue record of this book is available from the British Library

ISBN-10: 0335 22099 1 (pb)   0335 22100 9 (hb)
ISBN-13: 978 0335 22099 1 (pb)   978 0335 22100 4 (hb)

Library of Congress Cataloging-in-Publication Data
CIP data applied for

Typeset by RefineCatch Limited, Bungay, Suffolk
Printed in Great Britain by Bell & Bain Ltd, Glasgow
www.bell-bain.com

Mixed Sources
Product group from well-managed
forests and other controlled sources
www.fsc.org Cert no. TT-COC-002769
© 1996 Forest Stewardship Council

The *McGraw·Hill* Companies

To my family –
Marloes, Jeroen, Jessica and Dylan –
who make it all worthwhile

We aspire to a society that is not merely civil but is good. A good society is one in which people treat one another as ends in themselves. And not merely as instruments; as whole persons rather than as fragments; as members of a community, bonded by ties of affection and commitment, rather than only as employees, traders, consumers or even as fellow citizens. In terms of the philosopher Martin Buber, a good society nourishes 'I–Thou' relations, although it recognises the inevitable and significant role of 'I–It' relations.

The good society is an ideal. While we may never quite reach it, it guides our endeavours and we measure our progress by it.

The vision of a good society is a tableau on which we project our aspirations, not a full checklist of all that deserves our dedication. And the vision is often reformulated as the world around us changes, and as we change. Moreover, it points to different steps that different societies best undertake, depending on their place on the Third Way.

The Third Way is a road that leads us toward the good society. However, it should be acknowledged at the outset that the Third Way is indeed fuzzy at the edges, not fully etched.

But this is one of the main virtues of this approach: it points to the directions that we ought to follow, but is neither doctrinaire nor a rigid ideological system.

(*Amitai Etzioni* 2000)

Contents

Introduction

By background and temperament, I am a school improvement activist. Over the past 30 years or so I have self-consciously located myself at the intersection of practice, research and policy. It is here that I felt I could best contribute to the process of educational reform. Reflecting on this time, one of the initiatives I am most proud of is the work I did with the Improving the Quality of Education for All (IQEA) school improvement project, in which we collaborated with hundreds of schools in England and elsewhere in developing a model of school improvement and a programme of support. The IQEA approach aims to enhance student outcomes through focusing on the teaching–learning process as well as strengthening the school's capacity for managing change. More recently, however, I have found myself as a national policymaker, concerned not only with regional networks of schools, but also with part-responsibility for transforming a whole system. These two sets of experiences have convinced me that not only should every school be a great school, but also that this is now a reasonable, realizable and socially just goal for any mature educational system. This is the argument I pursue in the current volume.

It has been some time since I have, metaphorically, put pen to paper. That is explained simply – as a civil servant it was inappropriate for me to voice personal opinions in print. Having served a parliamentary term as chief adviser to three Secretaries of State – Estelle Morris, Charles Clarke and Ruth Kelly – I have now returned to an international role in educational leadership, where hopefully I can use this relatively unique experience to inform practice, policy and research in education. So, the personal purpose in writing this book is to give myself the opportunity to reflect on the dynamics of school improvement and change in light of my recent experiences.

As always, writing, even of the academic variety, is an exercise in biography. I have never made a secret of this and it is the same in this book. At one level, it represents an interpretation of my time in government, what I tried to achieve and what I learned. But it is no 'kiss and tell'. I was fortunate in middle age to have had the opportunity to play a minor role in one of the great reforming governments, in terms of education at any rate, anywhere in the world. Working with colleagues of such passion, commitment and intelligence was an enormous privilege. As a consequence, the detailed story of the 'cut and thrust' of life in government is irrelevant as compared with what was being achieved and what we attempted to achieve. That experience, however, has profoundly affected my thinking on education and it is that story that I tell in this book.

As I reflect on the evolution of my thinking about education over the past few years, many images crowd my mind. From this richness, I would just like to select five experiences or reflections as being indicative and character-istic of the way in which my attitudes deepened and strengthened during that time.

The first is, for those of you who know me, somewhat predictable. Late on Monday 27 April at Advanced Base Camp on the East Rongbuk Glacier on the north side of Mount Everest at 6450 metres, I sent, via satellite, the following message:

> *Friends,*
>
> *Earlier today, my son Jeroen (15) and I made an ascent of the North Col of Everest (7055ms almost 23,500ft). Our two companions Paul Sillitoe (service user) Bill Mumford (Chief Executive) from MacIntyre Care the charity for the mentally disabled reached their summit on the fixed ropes at c6725ms. Even so our group has made a little history – Paul has gone higher than any other mentally disabled person on Everest and Jeroen is probably the youngest person to reach the North Col.*
>
> *The North Col of Everest has iconic status in mountaineering. It pro-vided the initial platform for the early attempts on Everest in the between war period e.g. Mallory et al, and more recently has been the setting for some of the boldest climbing ever seen e.g. my friend Peter Boardman who died on ENE Ridge, Reinhold Messner's solo 3 day ascent of North Face, and Marco Siffredi's snow board descents and ultimate death on N Face.*
>
> *The ascent to the North Col finds a complex route through crevasses, over ice cliffs and between steep snow slopes. After helping Paul and Bill on their descent I struggled to catch up with Jeroen but he inevitably beat me to the top! Our descent down the fixed ropes with our Sherpa companions fortunately only took 2 hrs in the increasingly intense cold as compared to 7 hrs in the heat of ascent.*
>
> *A great adventure only made possible by our friend Russell Brice the premier High Altitude Guide. We begin our descent tomorrow and I'll have my feet back behind the Whitehall desk on Tuesday.*
>
> *As ever,*
> *David*

The reason for sending the message and for going to the north side of Everest in the first place was twofold. The first was to help Paul realize a dream; the second was to demonstrate, unequivocally, that people with disabilities such as Paul's can do remarkable things. It is this belief in the human potential – that most (if not all) can, under the right conditions, fulfil their potential – that keeps me and hundreds of thousands of other educators getting up in the morning. I also hope that it is this simple belief that has characterized what I have tried to achieve in the variety of roles that I have had the good fortune to occupy in my professional career.

The second experience is that of getting to know Paul Grant, head teacher of Robert Clack School, and then visiting the school in Barking and Dagenham, a borough in the east of London. These couple of paragraphs give an indication of the transformation achieved at Robert Clack.

> *Robert Clack School in Barking and Dagenham fell into a spiral of decline over a decade ago to become a 'very low achieving school'. It had all the attendant problems of such an inner city school, including: low expectations for student achievement, a poor environment, with graffiti and dilapidated buildings, very poor behaviour, with no clear system or responsibility taken by the head, a lack of direction, with ineffective leadership and little unity amongst staff and to cap it all, a significant financial deficit. Now, however, 68% of its students achieve 5 A*-Cs at GCSE, and the school received a grade 1 in every category of a recent Ofsted inspection despite serving an area where a high proportion of families live on low incomes.*
>
> *The catalyst for change was a new head teacher, who was promoted internally from a Head of Department post. The Local Authority felt that this was a significant risk but the Governors were convinced by his vision for the school. The Governors were right, and following his appointment the school sustained improvement over a decade or more. Although I do not have the space to describe what Paul Grant did there were four interrelated strategies that he pursued in the early days.*
> - *First, he established a clear vision for improvement that translated into both urgency and clear principles for action.*
> - *Second, he diagnosed existing strengthens and weaknesses and made appropriate actions to create early wins and boost staff confidence.*
> - *Third, he created a clear reform narrative that takes root in the school and is seen by the majority of staff to be consistently applied.*
> - *But above all, he put student achievement and professional learning at the heart of the process.*
> - *Second, he diagnosed existing strengthens and weaknesses and made appropriate actions to create early wins and boost staff confidence.*
> - *Third, he created a clear reform narrative that takes root in the school and is seen by the majority of staff to be consistently applied.*

- *But above all, he put student achievement and professional learning at the heart of the process.*

From this emerged a school where students were secure, proud and achieving, where staff were confident, collaborative and competent and where the school was gaining a reputation for excellence across the board locally nationally and internationally.

As someone who has spent much of his professional life attempting to understand the process of improvement in schools, I have been struck by how schools with similar intakes and resources and exposure to similar ideas and initiatives can appear initially superficially similar, yet produce such different outcomes in terms of ethos and expectations on the one hand, and learning and achievement, on the other. Why are some schools successful at improving themselves at a transformational level and others are not? Paul's example and that of many other heads we have been working with recently, have challenged me to understand the processes involved more deeply. The outcomes of this research will be published in due course. There will be a clear link between this and that book. The current volume lays out the argument for system leadership and the subsequent book describes its practice.

Parenthetically, in reflecting on my visit to Robert Clack I was reminded of a conversation I had had with a secondary head in Cardiff a number of years ago. In telling me of his inclusion policy, he shared with me what he said to those pupils that he accepted then, because no one else would have them. He took them into his room and said gently: 'The good news is that we love you – the bad news is that we will never let you go!' To me, this is the essence of inclusion and the foundation, as we shall see, of the Good Society.

The third experience, although individual, was very significant to the genesis of this book. It was one cold winter's night on a train travelling to the north of England and I was desperately trying to find the time to think through the structure of this book. At the encouragement of Tom Bentley I began to read Amitai Etzioni's *The Third Way to a Good Society*. I had spent much of the previous four weeks assembling a half draft of the book, which was supposed to argue to multiple audiences for a 'third way' for educational reform. I was attempting to formulate a strategy that was driven by social justice but that also gave freedom to schools to innovate, support one another and build lateral capacity within the system. I was looking for a common thread, a unifying thought and found it on reading Etzioni's monograph. I have quoted his definition of the Good Society and the Third Way in the opening pages of the book. My purpose in doing so, is to highlight the similarity between his general conception of the Good Society and its educational equivalent I propose in this book under the guise of 'every school a great school'. Similarly, the means of achieving it – the Third Way – corresponds to the educational strategy outlined here. In this further quotation, Etzioni points to community as the structural component necessary to achieve the Good Society; the educational equivalent, of course, is networking:

> *The ethical tenet that people are to be treated as purposes rather than only as means is commonly recognized. Less widely accepted is the significant sociological observation that it is in communities, not in the realm of the state or the market, that this tenet is best institutionalized.*
>
> *Equally pivotal is the recognition that only in a society where no one is excluded, and all are treated with equal respect, are all people accorded the status of being ends in themselves and allowed to reach their full human potential. Furthermore, the core communitarian idea – that we have inalienable individual rights and social responsibilities for each other – is based on the same basic principle: we are both entitled to be treated as ends in ourselves and are required to treat others and our communities in this way.*
>
> *The good society is one that balances three often partially incompatible elements: the state, the market and the community. This is the underlying logic of the statements above. The good society does not seek to obliterate these segments but to keep them properly nourished – and contained.*

For me this is the 'real deal'. The reciprocity between 'individual rights and social responsibilities' is at the heart of system leadership. This definition of community reflects the emphasis in this book on the key collaborative arrangements that will characterize the new educational landscape.

Now a word about epistemology. I say that deliberately and provocatively because it is important that you know where I am coming from. Epistemology is defined in my dictionary as the 'theory of method' or 'grounds of knowledge'. So it is important to declare what my theory of knowledge is, my theory of action. It is very simple. As I have already noted, for my entire professional life I have deliberately attempted to situate myself at the confluence of policy, practice and research. This has not always been a comfortable position to hold and, sadly, on occasions, has led to opposition from those who I would normally have regarded as allies in the quest for establishing the Good Society. But no worry, here we stand and one can do little else. I am still inspired by the words of Ernest Becker as he struggled to finish his final book before cancer extinguished that vibrant light. He wrote in the preface to *Escape from Evil* (1975) that:

> *As in most of my other work, I have reached far beyond my competence and have probably secured for good a reputation for flamboyant gestures. But the times still crowd me and give me no rest, and I see no way to avoid ambitious synthetic attempts; either we get some kind of grip on the accumulation of thought or we continue to wallow helplessly, to starve amidst plenty.*

So do I. I try in my own way to transcend policy, practice and research, to unify all three in the pursuit of educational excellence and the realization of human potential. Now that I am back in a university and my publications are subject to external review, I hope that the RAE panel will also view this as a legitimate place to locate one's scholarly work when they come to read this book.

Finally, I have recently been struck by Richard Elmore's felicitous if provocative phrase that 'education is a profession without a practice'. This is something that I have been saying far less elegantly for some time. This is not to say that there is not excellent practice in education – far from it. The problem as I see it is twofold. First, much of the outstanding teaching and leadership in schools is often tacit rather than explicit. Good teachers are good teachers because they are good teachers. It is an individual achievement rather than a consequence of a disciplined process of professional enquiry. In general, as educators we lack generalized 'theories of action' that link cause and effect in the pursuit of enhanced student learning through the exercise of articulated professional competence. It is not the paucity of individual excellence that is the problem – it is, rather, that this excellence is not commonplace; and it is not commonplace because we lack a language for professional communication and progress. It is this realization, however contentious it may seem, that explains the slow rate of improvement in many schools and systems. In those schools and systems however, where the practice of teaching and leadership is explicit shared and based on evidence, then progress by normative standards is unusually rapid and sustained. One of the purposes of this book is to contribute in a modest way to the development of an educational practice, at least in the areas of teaching and leadership.

These five reflections have been highly influential in conditioning my thinking as I have been developing the narrative of this book. The belief in the realization of human potential as seen on the Everest excursion with Paul Sillitoe; the power of transformational leadership as exemplified by Paul Grant; the need for educational reform to contribute to establishing the Good Society as identified by Etzioni; Becker's example of trying to make sense of it all; and Elmore's exhortation that one needs to contribute to the development of an 'educational practice' provide the subtext for much of what follows.

No book, however, is a singular achievement and certainly this is no exception. So, having spoken of the personal, let me now acknowledge some of the debts and obligations to those who have helped and supported me.

I am enormously grateful to Elpida Ahtaridou, Rob Higham and Tony Mackay who went beyond the bounds of professional commitment and friendship to help me with the hard work of translating my initially inchoate draft into something that makes some sort of sense. Whatever the result, it is their achievement as much as mine.

I am also most fortunate to enjoy a personal as well as professional friendship with many of the outstanding researchers and analysts in the field of education. I have learned much from them as is evident from the pages that follow. Among those whose writing and practice has had an impact on my recent thinking and practice, particularly as I thought through this book, are: Michael Barber, Tom Bentley, Brent Davies, Richard Elmore, Michael Fullan, Andy Hargreaves, David H. Hargreaves, Bruce Joyce, Ken Leithwood and Andreas Schleicher. The world of education is incomparably richer as a result of their accumulated wisdom.

My time in government was both exhilarating and formative, during which I learned a great deal. I have already commented on my colleagues' collective passion, intellect and commitment. Among those who proved outstanding role models and gave me extended tutorials in the 'dark arts' were: Christina Bienkowska, Charles Clarke, John Dunford, Mike Gibbons, Richard Harrison, Paul Higgins, Graham Last, Bruce Liddington, Andrew McCully, David Miliband, Estelle Morris, Ralph Tabberer, Ray Shostak and Frances and John Sorrell. Educational policy and the vision of the Good Society are safe in their hands.

I have continued to learn from my colleagues in schools whose example, altruism and power of practice is leading us inexorably towards imagining a radically different educational landscape. My mention earlier of Paul Grant was invidious, as is the following list, insofar as many others have similarly challenged my thinking and practice. I am, however, particularly grateful to: Yasmin Bevan, Trish Franey, Paul Grant, Sue Granville, Dexter Hutt, Vanessa Huws Jones, Alasdair Macdonald, Andy and Trish McCarthy, Hilary McKewan (decd), David Potter, Mary Richardson, Alan Roach, Kevin Satchwell, Mary Schofield (decd), Alan Steer, David Triggs and Michael Wilkins. These are the real system leaders. Thank you all for your insight and integrity.

Lastly, a word of explanation. In attempting to make a comprehensive argument for systemic reform, I inevitably had to draw on material I have published previously. In doing so, I have been as economic as possible and in each case used the opportunity to rewrite and update the text. I also need to acknowledge the Department for Education and Skills: some of the figures in the book are versions of those I originally commissioned whilst working in the Department. I was brought up in a nonconformist chapel in south Wales and learned from an early age that many may be the texts but all the sermons tend to be one.

There is little else to say in this introduction, apart from, perhaps, to reassure those of you who know me, my work and my family that all is well with us and that I remain in awe of my children's personalized learning journeys and what they are now teaching me.

David Hopkins
Harpenden, Herts, and Argentière, Mt Blanc
Summer 2006

PART 1
The context of system reform

The argument of the book is presented in miniature and the key concepts introduced. 'Every school a great school' is advanced as a heuristic for any social democratic educational system, the failings of previous large-scale reform efforts are analysed and an approach to system reform is presented as a radical alternative.

1 Every school a great school

Alan Bennett, in the introduction to his play *The History Boys* (2004) reflects somewhat pessimistically on what both he and I would most probably regard as being the true purpose of state education:

> *I'm old fashioned enough to believe that private education should long since have been abolished and that Britain has paid too high a price in social inequality for its public schools. At the same time, I can't see that public schools could be abolished (even if there was the will) without an enormous amount of social disruption. The proper way forward would be for state education to reach such a standard that private schools would be under-subscribed, but there's a fat chance of that, particularly under the present administration.*

I agree wholeheartedly with the aspiration – that every school should be great, but disagree profoundly with the prognosis – that there is a fat chance of this happening.

Ask any parent about the goal of educational reform and the answer is simple – why can't every local school be a great school? It's a no-brainer and there is ample evidence in support. Take for example:

- a poll conducted by *Which?* (2005) showing a staggering 95% of parents wanting access to high-quality local state schools
- the Policy Exchange's report that parents want an adequate supply of good school places (O'Shaughnessy and Leslie 2005)
- the statement from Margaret Morrissey, spokeswoman for the National Confederation of Parent Teacher Associations (NCPTA), that: 'Parents want to be absolutely sure that they are going to be able to get their children into a good local school' (NASUWT 2005)
- the Education and Skills Committee's (2004, 2006) belief that the vast majority of parents simply want a good local school

- interestingly, local schools are also generally rated highly in satisfaction surveys reflecting a desire for good local provision.

In light of this, Bennett's reference to the abolition of public schools is, I think, a red herring. This is particularly the case in the UK where independent schools account for just under 7% of the education of all children (Independent Schools Council 2006). I am also excited by the enthusiasm many independent schools are showing for collaborating with the maintained sector. No, the real question is – is it possible for every school to become great? My answer is that, by and large, this is now a realistic expectation.

The reason for my optimism is the recent success of educational reform efforts in many countries where increases in student learning are being sustained at high levels and where the achievement gap has been significantly reduced. So, for example, look at PISA results in 2000 and 2004, when in assessing reading, mathematical and scientific literacy showed that Finland, Norway, Canada, Japan and Korea sustained increases in student learning at high levels as well as significantly reducing the achievement gap. These countries are a great example of how to sustain high excellence and high equity where low socio-economic status (SES) students are not doomed to failure and deprivation does not remain the 'best' predictor of academic success.

In England, the success of both the primary and secondary national strategies and specific school-level interventions have, despite often poor publicity, significantly improved standards of student achievement and learning over the past 10 years. Although, as we shall see later, there is still much to be done before one could claim that the English educational system is transformed, progress has been such, and the learning from the experience sufficient, that there is now a high degree of clarity over what needs to be done to reach this goal.

I believe that because of the largely positive experiences of educational reform in the past quarter century, we are now close to what Malcolm Gladwell (2000) has called the 'tipping point'. He argues that every successful innovation that impacts on society has a 'tipping point' where the change transforms itself exponentially from enjoying a limited local or sectional interest to become a mass phenomenon. The 'tipping point' in education is being reached for two reasons. First, because every school becoming great is now a distinct possibility. Second, and probably more importantly, society, as the result of increasing information about the performance of the system, is not just demanding excellence, but is also prepared to take some responsibility for it happening. This is the real message of Gladwell's book. It is that when reform, instead of being imposed from above, becomes owned by those involved transformation really does occur. In the end, he says, tipping points are a reaffirmation of the potential for change and the power of intelligent action.

Seth Godin in *Unleashing the Ideavirus* (2001) argues in a similar vein. He claims, with Gladwell, that ideas have the potential to become contagious, but not at the behest of advertisers or politicians; like a virus they become contagious as a consequence of human interaction. Although the most successful ideaviruses sometime appear to be accidents, it is possible, Godin claims, by using a strategy such as the formula he proposes in his book, to dramatically increase the chances an ideavirus will spread. It is important to recognize, however, that an ideavirus loves a vacuum; the more crowded the marketplace the more difficult it will be for an idea to catch on. As Godin says, the race will go to the swift. He also emphasizes that once an ideavirus spreads, it follows a lifecycle. Ignore the lifecycle and the ideavirus dies out. Feed it properly and it will continue to blossom and spread for a long time.

Although Gladwell and Godin grounded their theories in social activity and marketing, their ideas do have a resonance for educational reform and change. They also come at an opportune time. It may well be that the system is currently becoming immunized to 'top-down' and command and control change strategies. Viewing the process of educational change as akin to the spreading of a positive and benign virus stands in stark contrast to the centre–periphery model of change that has been so dominant in the recent past. An approach to reform based on the principles of contagion, viruses and epidemics may now be the best way of disseminating and building a consensus for reform, as we seek a phase of educational change based on the principle of 'every school a great school'.

The purpose of this book is to contribute to the potential viral communication as an alternative approach to educational change. This shift from vertical to horizontal ways of working is, I believe, the only way in which every school will become great. The great irony that is explored in detail in this book, is that for this to become a reality, it requires not just an individual school improvement effort, as we became so used to in the 1980s and 1990s, but a system-wide response. This is the key to achieving successful educational reform in the new century.

So, in this introductory chapter:

- the concept of 'every school a great school' is described in a little more detail
- the political difficulties in achieving system-level reform are explored
- a model of school improvement that fits into the system-wide approach being advocated here is presented
- principles underpinning the approach to system reform are set out
- ten lessons for system reform are proposed
- and, finally, the key concepts necessary for system reform are introduced through reviewing the argument of the book as a whole.

'Every school a great school'

The phrase 'every school a great school', although not literally achievable, is certainly not a mere slogan. It is an aspiration, but it is more than that – it is a metaphor with an edge. The edge is provided by the evidence that schools in the most challenging circumstances can improve and the strategies used to realize this are both articulate and generalizable.

In one of our current research projects, using student performance and value-added data together with inspection judgements, we have identified schools that have displayed sustained improvement over time from an extremely low base and those who were 'coasting' (stuck at average performance with low value-added) and who made striking moves onto a new trajectory. We are also achieving a certain degree of clarity as to how these schools have improved and managed to sustain their improvement.

These schools, rather than being overwhelmed by external change, have made a sustained effort at building a positive culture for teaching and learning within the school. This is not to say that external reforms were not important; all the schools we are observing work gladly within the existing policy framework. The big difference is that they first ensured that the 'basics' were in place and then were selective in adapting external change for their own internal purposes. The important lesson here for policymakers is that enhancing teacher quality is more important than effecting structural change.

In looking at how schools have moved from being good to great and sustained their performance we were inspired by Jim Collins' book *Good to Great* (2001: 162, 168). He begins the book by arguing that 'good is the enemy of great' and continues by maintaining that 'we don't have great schools, principally because we have good schools'. By and large, he feels that we are content with being good and that is the main problem. Although Collins' research focused on companies rather than schools, there are some fascinating comparisons in terms of what 'great' companies are like and how they became 'great'. It is instructive to relate these two descriptions of great companies to those outstanding schools one is familiar with:

> *Enduring great companies don't exist merely to deliver returns to shareholders. Indeed, in a truly great company, profits and cash flow become like blood and water to a healthy body. They are absolutely essential for life, but they are not the point of life.*

And:

> *Enduring great companies preserve their core values and purpose while their business strategies and operating practices endlessly adapt to a changing*

world. This is the magical combination of 'preserve the core and stimulate progress'.

The image of schooling conjured up by these quotations is one of a school and classroom culture of high expectations where students realize their potential as a consequence of a rounded education rather than forced by teaching to the test. This occurs because, as in the second quote, the school has a belief in the learning potential of all students, understands cause and effect in terms of teaching and learning and innovates around these core beliefs and practices.

In terms of becoming 'great', Collins compared companies that were great (top performing and sustained improvement over some 15 years) with those that were by all the usual standards 'good'. He explained the difference by pointing to how the great companies made assiduous efforts to get the basics right before flirting with innovation.

For example, in relation to schools, I am sometimes asked: 'Would more teaching assistants or greater use of ICT ensure learning is tailored to student need?' Although these are legitimate questions, they are actually second-order questions. We must first establish a strong culture of teaching and learning, because with this in place teachers will then be best able to decide how to deploy more teaching assistants or use ICT – funded overall by the centre, but determined by informed professionals.

On this, I believe it is important to remember what Collins wrote:

> *None of the good to great companies began their transformations with pioneering technology, yet they all became pioneers in the applications of technology once they grasped how it fit [with their core improvement strategies] and after they hit breakthrough.*
>
> *The comparison companies frequently tried to create a breakthrough with large, misguided acquisitions. The good to great companies, in contrast, principally use large acquisitions after breakthrough, to accelerate momentum in an already fast spinning wheel.*

This is the approach being advocated here. As is seen later, it is the relentless focus on establishing the essentials of teaching and learning, in order to ensure that the basic organizational conditions are in place that lays the foundation for every school being great.

A final word on this. Of course I am not naive enough to believe that every school can become great in absolute terms. Life is not like that. I am using the phrase as a heuristic, a metaphor to describe the aspiration we should have for our educational system. I do, however, agree with Collins that the good is the enemy of the great; we have, for example, too many complacent and coasting schools in England. I also believe that every school should be on a trajectory to being great. We have sufficient diagnostics in the system to allow a robust analysis of where a school is at and we now know enough about the ingredients of successful schooling to allow an intelligent response.

If we now link the 'good to great' concept with the desire of parents to send their children to a local school then we have, as I have already intimated, a simple proposition for the guiding principal for educational reform – policies that ensure that every school is great. We discuss in the following section why many governments find this apparently simple proposal so difficult to respond to.

The challenge of system reform

For a country to succeed it needs both a competitive economy and an inclusive society. That requires an education system with high standards, which transmits and develops knowledge and culture from one generation to the next, promotes respect for and engagement with learning, broadens horizons and develops high expectations. We want to ensure that all young people progressively develop the knowledge, understanding, skills, attitudes and values in the curriculum and become effective, enthusiastic and independent learners, committed to lifelong learning and able to handle the demands of adult life. This is a pretty good description of an educational system committed to ensuring that every school is at least a good school and that most are on the journey to becoming great.

It is salutary to recognize, however, that whether the goal of 'every school a great school' is achieved or not, its realisation is more about professional and political will rather than strategic knowledge. It is now over 25 years since Ron Edmonds (1979) asked his felicitous question: 'How many effective schools would you have to see to be persuaded of the educability of all children?' He continued: 'We already know more than we need to do that. Whether or not we do it, must depend on how we feel about the fact that we haven't so far.' Edmonds was referring to the relative failure of students from ethnic backgrounds in inner city America. Our concern here stems from the same root – ensuring that every student, *irrespective of background*, achieves his/her potential. To achieve that for a society requires that every school succeeds for every student.

The aspiration of 'every school a great school', although easy to articulate, has, as Edmonds intimated, implications that challenge the resolve of many national and local governments. There seem to me to be at least three reasons why many governments find it difficult to take the phrase seriously and to regard it as more than empty rhetoric:

- First, *this is an avidly social justice agenda redolent with moral purpose and needs to be communicated as such.* Sadly, many of our leaders feel uncomfortable talking about values that have concrete outcomes. Yet, without this, one cannot build a consensus for social change.

- Second, *it places the focus of reform directly on enhancing teaching quality and classroom practice rather than structural change.* Government policy implementation has mostly used the school as the unit of intervention. Yet, international research evidence such as PISA shows that (a) the classroom is key in raising achievement and (b) the range of variation within any school dwarfs the difference between schools in the UK by a factor of three or four times.
- And third, *it requires a commitment to sustained, systemic change because a focus on individual school improvement always distorts social equity.* The evidence from the charter school movement in the United States and grant-maintained schools in England suggests that although such initiatives raise standards for those involved, they tend to depress standards in surrounding schools. This is not at all to argue against school autonomy, but to caution that it should be done within inclusive and collaborative settings.

These three challenges are of a different order. The first relates more to political will and belief, the second and third to strategy and educational understanding. All three, however, reflect the commitment that Edmonds so graphically refers to. And all three are necessary and need to act in a dependent relationship if every school stands a chance of becoming a great school. Last but not least, all three are necessary components of an educational version of a 'Third Way'. The equivalent of Etzioni's *Good Society* (2000) is the 'every school a great school' metaphor. Both are underpinned by a moral purpose.

Moral purpose is a plastic concept, but, for our initial purposes, I will define it as 'raising the bar and closing the gap' in terms of student learning and achievement. This, however, is a strictly educational definition and if we are serious about social justice and inclusion, then as educators we have a real challenge, because as Basil Bernstein (1970) said some 35 years ago: 'Education cannot compensate for society.' Although issues of politics and social change are beyond the scope of this book, it is worth reminding ourselves at this point that moral purpose in education needs to be seen in a broader context, even if at any one point in time we can do little about it.

In his new book, *Beyond Turnaround Leadership*, Michael Fullan (2006: 14) expresses the thought in this way:

> As we have seen, this is not just a matter of education policy and practice, but also of social and economic policies – all devoted to the same end: improving the social environment as the route to greater prosperity –

economically, as well as for our health and well-being. This puts education reform in perspective, and allows us to start with turning around schools, not as an end in itself, but rather as a tiny part of a more fundamental reform agenda.

Both Bernstein and Fullan express something that many people miss out; schools are not isolated from the world but they are a part of it. Changing only one part of a whole can have an impact, but not as much as if you change most or all of its parts, if needed, and make them work in complementary ways. This is why it takes more than reforms in education to reconstruct a society and more for them to actually work. A holistic approach to reform must take place with societal and economic policies complementing educational ones. This is how we can make a real difference. In this respect, educational reform is but part of societal reform, so educators must appreciate that they can only do so much – but having said that, if they cannot compensate for society they must redouble their efforts to do all they can to operate on the contexts they can influence – on the social and economic milieu that their students inhabit. Looked at another way, achieving moral purpose in education is much easier if there is political will behind it.

I was privileged to have some firsthand experience of this when serving as the Chief Adviser on School Standards in the Department for Education and Skills in England. The educational reform programme in England is discussed in more detail in the following chapter, but it is worth noting here the contribution visionary politicians can make to moral purpose and to establishing a 'Third Way'.

Despite the great educational reforms achieved by Labour governments in England (for example, the creation of the comprehensive school in the 1960s and the literacy and numeracy reforms in the 1990s), Labour has always been better at knowing what it was against rather than what it was for. It was not until Estelle Morris in her social market foundation speech (2002) and David Miliband in his speech on a social democratic education settlement in March 2003 that New Labour could claim to have had a guiding philosophy for its educational reforms. In brief, the main contours of Miliband's settlement were:

- A vision of educational purpose and practice based on the ambition of full and democratic citizenship for all.
- A commitment to teaching as a thinking and developing profession, with power devolved and accountability accepted.
- A strategy to equalize life chances by tilting against inequality, with innovation and collaboration to improve standards.
- Sufficient funding, devolved to school level and allocated to need.
- An understanding that culture matters as well as structure and the dominant culture needs to support educational advance.

He concluded the lecture by saying that:

> *Equal worth. Active learning. Informed professionalism. High expectations. These are the foundations of a new education settlement. The ultimate test is not that they hold firm for a few months, or even a parliamentary term, but that they endure.*

It was the commitment to this settlement that led to a more personalized and systemic approach to educational reform in England during New Labour's second term.

In this section I have attempted to discuss the broader political and policy implications of every school being a great school. There are three main conclusions. First, that education cannot compensate for society; second, that positive political support can take us a long way; and third, the preceding two points not withstanding, there is much that educators can do. It is to a framework for such an approach to school improvement that we now turn.

A model of school improvement

The experience of the 'good to great' schools that we are researching and briefly described earlier is highly consistent with the model of school improvement that evolved out of my work with the Improving the Quality of Education for All (2002) project. The model was described in detail in *School Improvement for Real* (2001) and although it has been refined in light of changing contexts the basic idea remains the same. It is that the context and process of school improvement can be expressed through the image of a series of concentric rings.

In the centre is personalized learning, which represents (a) the school's goal that every student will reach their potential and (b) a definition of achievement that embraces both standards and learning capability. A learning focus such as this will not only raise standards but will also reduce the range of performance in a school, thus simultaneously raising the bar and narrowing the gap.

The next ring is comprised of those essential ingredients of effective classroom practice necessary for personalized learning – the teacher's repertoire of teaching and learning strategies, the organization of curriculum content, the management of learning behaviour and assessment for learning.

Such classroom practice is found in schools that have organizational conditions supportive of high levels of teaching and learning. Some of the key elements of these conditions are found in Figure 1.1 – collaborative planning that focuses on student outcomes, staff development that is committed to the

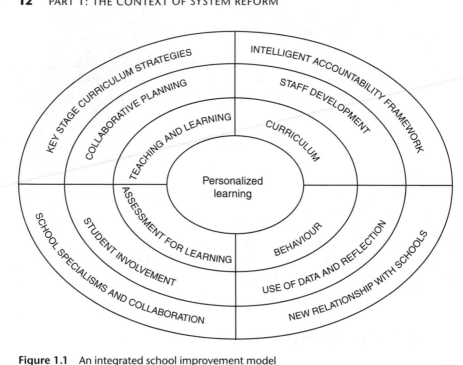

Figure 1.1   An integrated school improvement model

improvement of classroom practice, regular use of data, enquiry and reflection and the involvement of students in their own learning.

In today's educational systems, all of this activity normally takes place within the context of a centralized reform agenda – the outer ring. This is represented in the diagram by reference to a series of educational reforms such as the primary and secondary national strategies (formerly Key Stage 3 strategy) focusing on literacy and numeracy; the accountability framework including the new inspection system with sharper and shorter inspections and the promotion of school-based self-evaluation; the new relationship with schools which introduced the school improvement partners (SIP); and curriculum specialisms and collaboration sponsored by the Specialist School and Academies Trust.

When all the circles are pulling in the same direction, then the aspirations of school improvement have much more chance of success. All need to exist in a reciprocal relationship if student attainment is to be enhanced. The crucial issue is where the initiative for change and improvement comes from. As is seen in the following chapter, even the best of externally driven reform programmes envisage change comes from the 'outside – in'. The logic goes something like this: a high-quality policy or programme is developed and then implemented, with the assumption that it will impact on the school and be internalized through the school's planning processes, which, in turn, it is assumed will impact on classroom practices and through this will positively affect the learning and achievement of students.

Under this scenario even the most strategic and imaginative of policies only have a tenuous relationship with student learning and achievement. This concern is well caught in Michael Huberman's (1992: 11) graphic warning that:

> By not addressing the impact on pupils, we will have indulged in some magical thinking as before: that adoption meant implementation . . . that implementation meant institutionalisation . . . that enhanced teacher capacity means enhanced pupil achievement or development. . . . If changes in organisational and instructional practices are not followed down to the level of effects on pupils, we will have to admit more openly that we are essentially investing in staff development rather than in the improvement of pupils' abilities.

But even this sophisticated analysis is trapped within the logic of 'top-down' change. Huberman is arguing for an improvement in the strategies employed rather than turning the problem on its head. In those schools that have made the jump from 'good to great' the linear logic of policy implementation has been inverted. Instead of doing 'outside – in' better or more efficiently they start from the centre of the circle and move outwards; these schools begin at the other end of the sequence, with student learning. It is as if they ask: 'What changes in student learning and performance do we wish to see this year?' Having decided these, they then discuss what teaching strategies will be most effective at bringing this about and reflect on what modifications are required to the organization of the school to support these developments. Finally, they survey the range of policy initiatives confronting the school to see which they can most usefully mould to their own improvement plans.

Paradoxically, it is these schools that appear to be the most effective at interpreting the centralized reform agenda. Here, as we shall see in detail in the following chapter, reform is neither only system led nor only schools led, but necessarily both supporting each other. In other words, in the 'good to great' scenario:

- Schools exist in increasingly complex and turbulent environments, but the best schools 'turn towards the danger' and adapt external change for internal purpose.
- Schools use external standards to clarify, integrate and raise their own expectations.

- Schools benefit from highly specified, but not prescribed, models of best practice.
- Schools, by themselves and in networks, engage in policy implementation through a process of selecting and integrating innovations through their focus on teaching and learning.

At this point it is worth introducing briefly one of the key concepts in the book – the distinction between, on the one hand, 'large-scale' and, on the other, 'systemic' educational reform. In line with this discussion, 'large-scale' reform can be defined as change driven from the outside – in, where the metric for success is often regarded as annual increases in standardized test scores. We discuss in some detail the rise and fall of large-scale reform in the following chapter. Systemic reform, by way of contrast, occurs when there is a mutually supportive balance between 'outside – in' and 'inside – out' change with the emphasis being placed on capacity building, sustained improvement and personalized learning. It is reform based on substantive attention being given to linking together the three levels of the system – the classroom, the school and the system itself.

Principles for system reform

What has been implied in the preceding pages is that system change requires an entirely new approach to educational reform that has three key features:

- one that adopts a pedagogy designed to enable virtually every young person to reach his potential
- an approach to teaching that sees teachers as designers of increasingly powerful learning experiences
- the redesign of the landscape of schooling with independence and innovation and networking and lateral responsibility as its central characteristics.

This approach of system-level reform is territory that is not yet clearly charted. It is terrain, however, that is beginning to be explored by other educational change adventurers. The most prominent is the prolific Michael Fullan, who in three recent monographs (2003, 2005, 2006) has given us increasingly precise insights as to what the new landscape will look like. Readers of his work will therefore find many of the concepts discussed in this chapter familiar.

But there are two significant differences. The first is that Fullan refers to his 'tri-level solution', which is a similar idea to our three levels of classroom, school and system. Fullan's three levels, however, do not include a specific focus on the classroom but do distinguish between local and national system levels. Fullan also refers more generally to 'system thinkers' as a wider more encompassing role. In this book, we focus more on the head as the system leader but not to the exclusion of the broader 'system thinker' role. No one can claim to be a system leader unless they are also a system *thinker*. But these are differences of emphasis rather than substance and there is clear agreement on the need for agency and leadership for system reform.

When I was at the Department for Education and Skills in the UK, we developed a set of core principles to underpin this approach to transforming the educational system and act as a template against which to develop and evaluate our policies. Not only did we consult widely about these principles, we also tested them against both research and classroom evidence on best practice across the age range.

The following core principles are important in two respects. The first is that they provide evidence to support the authenticity of the model of school improvement used in this book. Many models claim some form of evidential basis, but few if any reflect state of the art knowledge at the confluence of research, policy and practice. Second, the principles reflect a new way of thinking about change that capture the reality of those schools that have moved from good to great. Ensuring that every school is a great school is not the consequence of either 'top-down' or 'bottom-up' change. As we shall see in the following chapter, the experiences of the last half century of educational reform suggest that neither works. Rather we are learning that both have to be in balance, in a reciprocal and lateral relationship for system-wide reform to become a reality.

For our purposes here the principles are presented in summary form moving from teaching and learning, through school improvement, to system-wide reform. This image is captured in Figure 1.2.

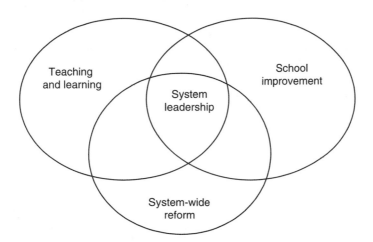

Figure 1.2 Core principles for system-wide reform

Policies to support learning and teaching should:

- *Set high expectations and show commitment to learner's success* by raising their aspirations and, where appropriate, gaining the support of parents or carers.
- *Establish what learners already know and build on it* by setting clear and appropriate learning goals, explaining them, and creating secure foundations for subsequent learning.
- *Structure and pace the learning experience to make it challenging and enjoyable* by using a variety of teaching methods and creating learning opportunities within and beyond the classroom.
- *Inspire learning through passion for the subject* by making it relevant to wider contexts and other subjects and to the learners' wider goals and concerns.
- *Make individuals active partners in their learning* by building respectful teacher/learner relationships and using assessment for learning – student self-assessment and metacognition – and these to inform subsequent planning and practice.
- *Develop learning skills and personal qualities* and particularly the ability to think systematically, manage information, learn from others and help others learn, together with confidence and self-discipline.

Policies to support school improvement should:

- *Focus systematically on teaching and learning* with leadership at all levels concentrating on raising standards and ensuring a rich curriculum for all and with plans for development that are supported across and beyond the school.
- *Base improvement activity* on qualitative and quantitative evidence on learners' progress, motivation, needs and satisfaction and selecting priorities and setting goals through rigorous audit and evaluation of this evidence against benchmarks.
- *Built collective ownership and develop leadership* by creating an improvement team drawn from across the organization and developing the skills of leading and managing change at all levels.
- *Engage in collaboration* with schools and colleges, community partners and other professional services that have strong mutual interests to widen the vision, increase resources and give access to new ideas and good practice.
- *Create time for staff to share good practice* through collective enquiry, peer observation and coaching in order to make their performance consistent and effective across the curriculum.
- *Embed improvement in the organization's systems and practices* by making

consequential changes to spread the impact of the work and so making the improvement process self-sustaining

Policies for system-wide reform should aim to:

- *Be based on clear values – a commitment to the success of every learner –* with a 'high-performance, high-equity' education system delivering personalized learning and teaching skills developed by high-quality initial training and career-long continuing professional development.
- *Develop a system that is coherent for learners at every level* by reflecting a clear and consistent strategic vision and organized to facilitate learning progression with appropriate choice of learning pathways.
- *Build frontline capacity* by devolving funding to the local and aim for a system that is steadily transformed by leaders and teachers, supported by government.
- *Establish an intelligent accountability framework* with clear national standards, ambitious targets, tests that support assessment *for* as well as *of* learning, inspection and transparent accountability based on sound data and incentives to raise achievement of all learners, support children at risk and celebrate success.
- *Strengthen diversity, collaboration and innovation* by encouraging every school or college to aspire to be a centre of excellence with a distinct ethos and mission, extend choice, spread excellence and drive innovation.
- *Develop local and regional capacity for professional support and challenge* by working strategically in partnership with national agencies, LEAs and other 'middle-tier' structures, higher education institutions as well as supporting and challenging leaders to improve continuously.

Unfortunately, few if any national education policies are informed by principles such as these. This may account for the lack of systemic reform seen in most countries. Indeed, my hypothesis would be that without a commitment to system reform and the integration of the three levels it is impossible to ensure that every school is a great school.

Ten lessons for system reform

My experience as a senior policy adviser as well as my reflections on a range of policy initiatives in many countries have led me to formulate a number of 'lessons for system reform'. They are an attempt to capture succinctly some of the traps to be avoided if any system is serious about raising both standards and opportunity for all. They have also been ordered in such a way as to reflect the key themes developed in each chapter or section of the book:

1 *The length of a school's development plan is in inverse proportion to its impact on practice* – reflects the idea developed in the introduction that it is the school's internal capacity rather than bureaucratic procedures that underpins its ability to raise and sustain standards in student achievement and learning.

2 *That for every school to become a great school, requires not an individual school improvement effort but a system-wide response* – this is the great irony explored in this chapter and becomes a key assumption underpinning the book.

3 *In the quest for social justice (and high excellence as well as high equity) neither top-down nor bottom-up change strategies work* – this truism, which now has wide research and practical support, provides the springboard for lateral capacity building and systemic reform approaches described in Chapter 2.

4 *Effective classroom experiences offer our children opportunities to explore and build important areas of knowledge, develop powerful tools for learning, and live in humanizing social conditions* – these are the essential conditions for personalizing learning as described in Chapter 3.

5 *The professional development of teachers is simultaneously the worst problem and best solution in education* [1] – this statement recognizes the fact that because teaching lacks a 'practice' it is still in its 'mediaeval age' and that before it can truly be called a profession, teachers' classroom practice needs to characterized by the expansion of repertoire and disciplined by evidence, the key themes discussed in Chapter 4.

6 *It is a recognition that isolation is the enemy of improvement, collaboration often the route to it, and that in gaining the benefits of collaboration diversity is a strength not a weakness* (Miliband 2003) – the point here is that an effective lateral system requires confident schools collaborating from positions of professional strength and competence, which is the basis of the approach to networking taken in Chapter 5.

7 *The margin of error within any national system of testing is always greater than the year-on-year increase in test scores demanded by politicians* – this somewhat contentious statement is the result of too close an acquaintance with the national testing system when I was a senior civil servant and informs the approach taken to intelligent accountability in Chapter 6.

8 *Moral purpose in education is best defined as a resolute failure to accept context as a determinant of academic and social success* – acting on

---

[1] With acknowledgement to Michael Fullan.

context and not accepting poverty and social background as necessary determinants of success in schooling is at the heart of the systemic approach to school transformation described in Chapter 7.

9   *In terms of school reform, leadership is to this decade what standards were to the 1990s* [2] – this adaptation of Michael Fullan's happy phrase reflects the discussion in Chapter 8 of system leadership as the meta-strategy for ensuring every school is a great school.

10   *Education needs its own 'grand unifying theory'* – much as the development of macroeconomic models in the post-World War Two period brought order and coherence to the debates on economic strategy. So, in Chapter 8 it is argued that the development of an analytic framework that capitalizes on the natural variation in educational performance observed across countries offers a similar prize in the arena of education policy.

Although the 10 lessons for system reform give an indication of what follows, it may be useful in the next and concluding section to review the content of the book in a little more detail.

Overview of the book

The purpose of this chapter has been to present the argument of the book in miniature and introduce some of the key concepts. The phrase 'every school a great school' has been advanced as a metaphor for the key educational goal of any social democratic educational system, a model of school improvement has been proposed, the failings of previous large-scale reform efforts have been hinted at and an approach to system reform as a radical alternative has begun to be advocated.

It will be argued in Chapter 2 that in many countries large-scale efforts at educational reform have, despite early success, largely stalled. In most cases, impressive early gains in student outcomes were followed by a 'plateauing' of results. An analysis of these large-scale reform efforts concludes that over time national prescription needs to be balanced by schools leading reform. The shift from prescription to professionalism, however, requires a systemic perspective – the building of capacity at all levels. Models of how such system reform can be achieved and how the plateau can become a springboard to sustained improvement will be presented.

In order to build capacity, while at the same time continuing to raise standards of achievement and learning, it is necessary that numerous national initiatives are replaced with a consensus on a limited number of educational

---

[2] Again, with acknowledgement to Michael Fullan.

trends. There are four key drivers to deliver 'every school a great school' and they provide the substance of the following four chapters. Here the emphasis of the book changes and the focus shifts to learning, teaching and school-level processes rather than discussions of policies designed to support school-level change. This is consistent with the argument of the previous two chapters that in order to sustain improvement reform needs to be systemic with schools in the vanguard.

In Chapter 3, it is argued that personalization is the guiding motif that allows a system to evolve from one based on delivery of services to one that emphasizes mass customization and co-production. Personalized learning is its educational form. This emphasis provides a bridge from prescribed forms of teaching, learning skills, curriculum and assessment to an approach to classroom practice that is predicated on enabling every student to reach his/her potential. The various pedagogic, assessment and curricular tools and procedures that allow teachers to personalize learning for all their students are described.

Personalized learning requires a radical readjustment to the way in which teachers teach and schools organize themselves. Teachers need to move to a new phase of professionalism, where they become increasingly focused and accountable for the way in which they use data and evidence to apply a rich repertoire of teaching models in order to personalize learning for all of their students. This *informed professionalism*, which is the focus of Chapter 4, implies radically different forms of professional development with a strong focus on coaching and modelling, which in itself requires a whole-school approach to staffing, timetabling and the deployment of an increasingly differentiated staffing model.

The recent history of educational reform is unequivocal as to the need for a degree of national prescription in its early stages. The argument of the book is that this balance needs to be sensitively adapted according to context. In the move from 'prescription' to 'professionalism', however, any accountability framework needs to be able not only to fulfil its original purpose, i.e. raising standards, but also to build capacity and confidence for professional accountability. How the concept of the 'accountability' evolves through the phases of system development and in the process becomes increasingly intelligent provides the focus for Chapter 5. The argument is that to be 'intelligent' any accountability system needs to balance both internal and external forms of assessment, hence the attention given in this chapter to the nature of formative assessment and the pivotal role of school self-evaluation.

Sustained educational improvement is not just the achievement of the school, its teachers and leaders. Sustained system improvement requires a vision of education that is shared and owned well beyond the school gates. This is the focus of Chapter 6. Ideally, an educational vision becomes part of the societal 'Zeitgeist' and conditions (high) expectations throughout society, which are then reflected in their own local conditions. The development of a guiding coalition at various levels of the system provides the essential building block. The various ways in which networks of schools can stimulate and spread innovation as well as 'opt out' of local control is advanced, and the way in which they would collaborate to provide curriculum diversity, extended services and professional support is described.

Leadership and the four drivers provide the essential building blocks for both ensuring high standards and building capacity in individual school settings. In Chapter 7, however, it is argued that for every school to be great, there is a need to move to scale through the realization that dynamic systems grow and develop by building on their inherent diversity and innovation. An approach to analysing system diversity and building on the inevitable segmentation of schools is proposed, as is a highly differentiated approach to school intervention based on the 'inverse proportion to success' principle. The focus is then placed on the need for leadership to move the system from one of national prescription to one where professionalism provides the energy and force for sustainability. This is essentially an adaptive challenge where progress requires new ways of thinking and operating. Mobilizing people to meet adaptive challenges, then, is at the heart of leadership practice. System leadership is proposed as an approach that builds on previous approaches, but that takes seriously the need to see leadership inside a problem-solving context that has both classroom understanding and system aspiration. The challenges and capacities of such leaders are described as is the moral purpose inherent in their role.

In Chapter 8, I conclude the book by reiterating that for every school to be great there are a small number of big ideas such as personalization, professionalism, networking, intelligent accountability, segmentation and system leadership, which, if employed intelligently and owned by those closest to the action, will realize the potential of system reform. The key to this is seeing system leadership as a way of transcending adaptive challenges and in so doing creating their own school futures. The key point being made in this chapter, however, is that the role played by national and local government needs to change to support this development. They have an important part to play in the new educational landscape, but it is of a different order than currently. We discuss some aspects of what this could be and point towards a (third) way in which school leaders, teachers, policymakers and the community can work together to make 'every school a great school' a reality.

2 From large-scale change to system-wide reform

In the early 1990s the first, and seemingly, at the time, the last words on the future of large-scale reform were those of Milbrey McLaughlin (1990: 11). On the basis of her reanalysis of the extensive Rand Change Agent study originally conducted in the United States during the 1970s, she wrote:

> *A general finding of the Change Agent study that has become almost a truism is that it is exceedingly difficult for policy to change practice, especially across levels of government. Contrary to the one-to-one relationship assumed to exist between policy and practice, the Change Agent study demonstrated that the nature, amount, and pace of change at the local level was a product of local factors that were largely beyond the control of higher-level policy makers.*

In asserting that 'policy does not mandate what matters', McLaughlin had captured the Zeitgeist, where both researchers and practitioners, for very different but predictable reasons, were arguing against the role of national policy in educational reform. In support and somewhat spuriously, both sides pointed to the insignificant impact on levels of student achievement that the dramatic increase in educational reform efforts in most western countries was having.[1] The attention turned to issues of local implementation.

Despite the orthodoxy established, and the legitimacy given by McLaughlin's dictum, in the middle of the 1990s increasing attention was again being given by both researchers and policymakers to 'moving reform to scale' (Elmore 1995a; Slavin and Madden 1999). Fullan's (2000: 20) review of district, whole-school and state reforms not only argued that 'large-scale reform had

---

[1] The failure of recent reforms to accelerate student achievement in line with policy objectives has been widely documented (e.g. Sebring et al. 1996; Rinehart and Lindle 1997; Hopkins and Levin 2000).

returned', but it also promised success if the following eight different factors were addressed:

- upgrade the system context
- become preoccupied with coherence making in the service of instructional improvement and student learning
- establish plenty of crossover structures
- downward investment/upward identity
- invest in quality materials (instruction and training)
- integrate pressure and support (set target/build capacity)
- get out of implementing someone else's reforms agenda
- work with systems.

I reviewed much of this evidence in School Improvement for Real (Hopkins 2001: Chapter 10). I suggested there that most governments now identify targets for achievement in key learning areas and, if these targets are to be realized, central policies need to incorporate three further elements:

- The first is making available to schools and local agencies strategies to assist them in realizing the goals they have identified, bearing in mind that all schools are at different levels of effectiveness.
- Second, if this could be achieved – a range of policy options related to programmes that have evidence of effectiveness – then schools could begin to select from among a range of options those strategies that address the particular targets they have set and the learning needs of their students.
- Third, government would then be in a position to target funding to those schools in the greatest need with far more secure knowledge. This way the goals the system as a whole had set itself would be achieved.

There is good evidence for example from the work of both Robert Slavin and Nancy Madden (2006) and the Success for All Foundation (2006) that such an approach can positively affect the progress in literacy of millions of young people.

At around the same time many national and local governments were advocating programmes commonly called 'performance-based reform' in an effort to raise standards across local and regional boundaries. As we shall see later on in this chapter, the general approach was to set targets for performance and then hold schools responsible for meeting them. This was a far less sophisticated approach to raising standards than the approach described in the previous paragraph and predictably had little positive impact on student achievement.

At the turn of the century, therefore, there was confusion over the viability of large-scale reform. On the one hand, national governments felt they could not leave educational improvement simply to local initiatives. On the other, avidly top-down approaches to reform based on short-term target setting were not yielding much success either. To some it was becoming clear that neither 'top-down' nor 'bottom-up' was working and that a more lateral approach to educational reform was needed if the nirvana of 'every school a great school' were to be realized. It was out of this debate that the approach to what we are calling here 'system reform' was beginning to develop. It was a belief that large-scale change could be achieved and be sustainable, not by following the linear logic of 'top-down' or 'bottom-up' but, rather, by developing an approach that built on the best of both with a common commitment to system-wide improvement.

The purpose of this chapter is to provide a sustained argument for 'system-wide reform', keeping in mind the logic of the previous chapter as being the only way in which every school can become great. This is in contrast to 'top-down' approaches to large-scale change, which, as the title of this chapter implies, has conspicuously failed to produce a sustained rise in standards. Perversely, I will also attempt to refute the McLaughlin (1990) position that a national vision for excellence cannot impact on the progress of individual students. In pursuing the argument, I will:

- review the basis and failure of the performance reform movement as well as the lessons to be learned
- describe the beginnings of the argument of the movement towards 'system reform' as the means of achieving every school becoming a great school
- refer in detail to the experience of primary schooling in England as a case study of large-scale system reform
- use the English primary example as one of the tension between 'informed prescription' and 'informed professionalism'
- conclude by clarifying the central policy conundrum of balancing national prescription with schools leading reform, and identifying the four key drivers that underpin system change.

The failure of performance-based reform [2]

We have already discussed in general the failure of large-scale performance-based reform to sustain improvements in educational standards. It is worth briefly looking at some of the evidence and to understand why such politically

[2] See Chapter 10 in Hopkins, D. (2001) *School Improvement for Real*. London: Routledge/Falmer.

important and initially at least often well-funded initiatives failed. Ken Leithwood and his colleagues (1999: 8) have reviewed the impact of a number of 'performance-based' approaches to large-scale reform. They identified seven specific properties of 'performance-based' approaches to reform:

1   a centrally determined, unifying vision and explicit goals for student performance based on the vision
2   curriculum frameworks and related materials for use in accomplishing the goals set for students
3   standards for judging the quality or degree of success of all students
4   coherent, well-integrated policies that reinforce these ambitious standards
5   information about the organization's (and especially the students') performance
6   a system of finance and governance that devolves to the local school site responsibility for producing improvements in system and student performance
7   an agent that receives information on organizational performance, judges the extent to which standards have been met and distributes rewards and sanctions, with significant consequences to the organization for its success or failure in meeting specified standards.

This approach to centralized educational change has become widespread over the past 10 years. The Leithwood review (1999: 40, 61–63) examined in a comparative manner five cases of performance-based reform that are well known and have been widely documented – Kentucky, California, New Zealand, Victoria (Australia) and Chicago. On the basis of this review, two striking conclusions were reached:

- The first is that on the available evidence there was no increase in student achievement in any case except Chicago and even that was 'slow in coming'.
- The second is 'the disappointing contribution that performance-base reforms have made to improving the core technology of schooling'. In particular these reforms did not:
  - adequately acknowledge local context
  - take the school site seriously
  - find incentives that work
  - contribute to significant increases in professional capacity
  - address and diagnose opportunity costs.

Although the impact of large-scale reform on student achievement is notoriously fickle, the fact that these reform strategies neglected to focus on teaching and learning and capacity building must have contributed to their inability to impact positively on student achievement.

The analysis of 'performance-based' approaches and the school district examples are entirely consistent with previous research on the implementation of large-scale reform efforts. As we have seen, evidence from the United States of major multi-site research studies[3] all points to the same conclusion. Unless central reforms address the context of teaching and learning, as well as capacity building at the school level, within the context of external support, then the aspirations of reform will never be realized. In support of this argument we will look in the following section at some of the evidence where large-scale reforms have had some positive and sustained impact.

From large-scale change to system-wide reform [4]

In the previous section we documented some examples of the failure of large-scale reform and suggested some reasons why. In the lexicon of the previous chapter this was because most of these efforts were predicated on a simplified 'outside – in' model. They were clearly technocratic in style assuming in Shaw's memorable phrase that 'change can be achieved by brute sanity'. Yet, the crude form that this approach has largely taken – the setting of targets linked to schemes of external accountability – ignored context and the need to build capacity and were narrow rather than systemic in approach. In developing the argument for system reform, it is instructive to search for examples of large-scale change that embrace these systemic characteristics.

In doing this and drawing on cases from around the world, including those from developing countries, I will also be making another important point that is implicit throughout the book. It is that despite culture and context, the language of system change is becoming increasingly global. This is not to say that a systemic change strategy can be transferred unthinkingly from one setting to another. It is to say, however, that the regularities of teaching and learning, of school organization, networking and leadership have relevance across cultures but of course need to be adapted to context. It is as if the ingredients of systemic change are globally similar but the recipe has to be mixed differently for differing situations. This maxim applies equally to schools and to systems. If this hypothesis is correct, then it should lead to a more intelligent worldwide debate about education reform, a theme

---

[3] Such as the Rand Study in the 1970s (see MacLaughlin 1990), the DESSI study (see Crandall et al. 1986) and the analysis of a range of restructuring programmes during the 1990s by Stringfield and his colleagues (1996).

[4] See Hopkins, D. (2001) *School Improvement for Real*. London: Routledge/Falmer.

that I return to in the final chapter of the book. Here we will look at some examples of successful system change to see whether this emerging hypothesis is confirmed.

There are a number of examples from the research on school districts in North America that illustrate that, under the right conditions, significant and rapid progress can be made in enhancing the learning of students. It is clear from these examples that unless centralized policies incorporate a focus on the context of teaching and learning, as well as capacity building at the school level, within the context of external support, then the aspirations of reform will never be realized. In support of this position two cases of successful school districts in California and Ontario, Canada, will be briefly described.[5]

Case 1: instructionally effective school districts in California

Those school districts in California that showed high performance on measures of student achievement display four common strategic characteristics:

1   The districts strongly espoused values that typically focused on:
    • improvement of student learning as the central goal
    • a positive approach to problem solving in the face of unforeseen difficulties
    • a view of structures, accountability and data as instruments for improvement rather than as ends in themselves
    • a heavy internal focus on the demands of teaching, rather than a focus on events in the external environment.
2   Despite strong leadership, these districts were less bureaucratic than their counterparts. They tended to rely more on a common culture of values to shape collective action than on bureaucratic rules and controls.
3   These districts showed a much greater clarity of purpose, a much greater willingness to exercise tighter controls over decisions about what would be taught and what would be monitored as evidence of performance, and a greater looseness and delegation to the school level of specific decisions about how to carry out an instructional program.
4   Superintendents in high-performing districts were:
    • knowledgeable about who were the key initiators of changes in curriculum and teaching strategies

---

[5] The California school district case is taken from Chapter 2 in Elmore, R.F. (2004) *School Reform from the Inside Out*. Cambridge, MA: Harvard University Press.

- active in monitoring curriculum and teaching in classrooms and schools, as well as active in the supervision, evaluation and mentoring of principals
- also more likely to relieve principals of their duties on the basis of their performance.

Case 2: literacy and numeracy in Ontario

Fullan (2006) describes eight interlocking strategies currently being put in place in Ontario in order to raise standards in literacy and numeracy across the province.

A guiding coalition

Establishing a guiding coalition (GC) of a small number of key leaders who consistently communicate among themselves and with all other stakeholders. In Ontario, they have the same message which is 'capacity building with a focus on results' through all eight strategic elements.

Peace and stability

A deliberate part of the strategy is to address the 'distractors'. A distractor is anything that takes one away from the continuous focus on teaching and learning and student achievement. Closing the gap is a system problem that needs a system solution that you cannot get if people are constantly sniping at each other.

The Secretariat for Literacy and Numeracy

Ontario chose to focus on literacy and numeracy in order to get the key foundational literacies established. Because capacity building (knowledge, resources and motivation necessary to improve literacy and numeracy) is a core part of the overall strategy, the Secretariat for Literacy and Numeracy was created.

Negotiating aspirational targets

Targets can be controversial. The goal in Ontario is to negotiate targets with each of the 72 districts by discussing starting points and negotiating next year's target as part of rolling reform.

Capacity building

Capacity building is multifaceted because it involves everything that affects new knowledge, skills and competencies; enhanced resources; and stronger commitments. Capacity building means something because there are so many concrete examples of it in practice. People know it and value it because they are experiencing it.

Growing the financial investment
Even though Ontario was in a serious budget deficit situation when the new government came into power, the premier made it clear that education and education spending was a priority.

Evolving positive pressure
Positive pressure is non-pejorative at the outset, treats people with respect and dignity, appreciates and is empathetic to challenging circumstances, provides assistance and support in the form of resources and capacity building, helps take all excuses off the table and then, in cases of persistent low performance, tough, decisive action is taken right away.

Connecting the dots with key complementary components
One cannot do everything at once, but as progress is made, it is necessary to begin working on other key components that surround literacy and numeracy, for example, 'well-being', high school reform, early childhood, teacher education and leadership development.

These eight strategic components are currently being coordinated and implemented in Ontario. The early results are promising. In terms of student achievement, taking Grade 6 reading as the example, after being flatlined below 60% proficiency for five years prior to 2003–2004, there was an increase of 2% in 2003–2004 and a further 5% in 2004–2005. Sub-analyses confirm that relevant gaps are closing slightly such as between low- and high-performing districts, low- and high-performing schools, boys and girls, as everyone moves up.

As these two cases are from North America, it is worth briefly looking at experience in less developed systems. One of the few authoritative and wide-ranging studies of educational change in developing countries is that reported by Per Dalin (1994). This book reports on World Bank-sponsored research that was carried out from 1987 to 1992 in 31 primary schools in Colombia, Ethiopia and Bangladesh. Dalin notes (1994: p. XVII) that prior to the How Schools Improve study many people assumed that there were certain 'obvious truths' about reform as:

- reforms should be incremental and gradual rather than wide-ranging
- tight inspection and control are essential for success
- the issue is designing a reform and its materials so well that it can be implemented faithfully and well with minimal training and assistance; in other words teachers are 'consumers' of new reform ideas
- success depends mainly on the quality of the reform ideas
- schools in general are resistant to reforms
- either 'top-down' or 'bottom-up' strategic work – depending on the educational context referred to.

Dalin claims that all these 'obvious truths' have been shown to be false, both in the How Schools Improve study as it relates to developing countries and in other recent large-scale studies of educational reform in industrialized countries.

This is a similar finding to the analysis I did of the Aga Khan East African school improvement initiative (Hopkins 2002a). The six projects I reviewed provide a unique insight into a sustained effort to build school improvement capacity and enhance student learning and attainment in a developing educational context. They reflect an evolving school improvement programme based on a coherent set of design principles that contain certain distinctive and possibly contentious features. There are six key principles that underlie the designs of each of the projects, that taken together, enhance the chances for improving the quality of teaching and learning in schools. The six principles are:

- school based
- whole school as unit of change
- ongoing professional development of teachers
- attend to school management and other organizational conditions
- prepare for institutionalization and sustainability
- involve stakeholders.

It was clear that the projects of the six projects were broadly based on these principles, the other more contentious feature of the Aga Khan approach to school improvement are the four strategies common to most of the school improvement projects. These four strategies are:

- investment in district-level teacher development personnel
- emphasis on enhancing teacher's general pedagogical expertise
- a focus on the adoption and use of child-centred activity-oriented (personalized) methods of teaching and learning
- promotion of data-based decision making for school development.

It is these strategies that make the Aga Khan approach to school improvement distinctive and coherent. The main strength of the initiative is that it focuses on the crucial lacuna in large-scale reform initiatives: the lack of attention to capacity building. What the Aga Khan initiative recognized that most 'performance-based reforms' currently do not, is that improvement will not be sustained over time without investing in the learning and development of teachers and their schools. In this respect, the Aga Khan initiative was well in advance of its time and provides a powerful example of tackling head-on the formidable challenges provided by systemic change.

Finally, in this review of successful systemic examples of educational reform, it is instructive to look at the case of Finland, the country that has consistently scored highly in the Programme for International Student Assessment (PISA) comparison of student achievement and so must have something going for it! It is important to note that in Finland there is support for education from all levels of society including the working classes. This is related to the role that education played in forming and promoting the Finnish national identity, as, after it gained and maintained its independence from Russia and the Soviet Union, education is seen as the means for national and individual advancement. It is the relative classless nature of this society and its greater levels of stability, trust and consensus resulting from this which lead to support for education. The following are some of the conclusions drawn from a visit to Finland made while I was working for the Department of Education and Skills:

- *High achievement at the bottom.* Finland's success in PISA rankings is due mainly to the spectacular performance of its lowest performing pupils in comparison to those of other highly ranked countries. The performance of its highest achieving pupils is not spectacular. There is also very low between-school variation.
- *Teaching is a popular career choice.* From surveys of young people's career aspirations, 26% of young people have teaching as their first-choice profession – universities are able to select the best of the best students for educations studies and teacher training (teacher's pay is at Organisation for Economic Co-operation and Development (OECD) average – probably lower than UK levels).
- *Highly educated teachers.* All teachers are educated to master's level, which includes a research thesis. Teachers in kindergarten only need a bachelor's degree. Teachers learn about research methods as a part of initial teacher training. Through this they acquire an appreciation of research and its place in informing professional development.
- *Small classes in lower years and small schools.* Class sizes appear to be much smaller the lower the grade: classes of 6–20 seemed common for grades 1–5 with low teens being the norm. At age 16+ classes appeared to be of 16–20 but could be of 30+. Schools seemed to have between 250 and 350 pupils at all age levels.
- *High level of special needs provision.* About 6% of pupils have full-time special needs support with about 20% of pupils have part-time special needs support. This provision has roughly doubled over the past nine years. Special needs provision is greatest for children in the first two years reflecting a belief that the provision of this support early on prevents greater problems developing later in a pupil's schooling.
- *Widespread involvement in and ownership of the curriculum.* National goals and norms are set centrally with details developed by municipalities and schools through flexible interaction between these

players. Teachers are valued as experts in curriculum development with the curriculum seen more as a process than a product and have a central role in school improvement. This results in schools and teachers owning the curriculum rather that feeling it is imposed. At a school level there is emphasis on developing pupils' skills to value each other, on learning how to learn and taking responsibility for their learning. The curriculum has to conform to national guidelines but is formulated and adapted to local contexts.

- *Trust is at the heart of the system.* It is assumed that teachers and schools will do the best possible for their pupils and they are trusted to do this. School inspection was abolished in the 1970s and there is no nationwide testing of all pupils until age 19 for matriculation exams. There is testing of a sample of schools at age 16. Results are shared with the schools and municipalities (average pop. of 12,000) to inform their self-evaluation but are not published. Trust and cooperation are an important part of Finnish society and that it has high levels of social capital. The question is: how far is new educational success a reflection of this social capital and homogeneity rather than excellence in teaching?

These examples from a range of both developing and developed systems provide a striking contrast to the previous discussion of performance-based reform. They begin to provide a specification for system-wide reform that is large scale yes, but also enhances standards of learning and achievement over time while building capacity and ownership throughout the system. My summary of these examples suggest that successful system-wide programmes:

- Have clarity of moral purpose focused on narrowing the achievement gap and ensuring all learners achieve their potential – rhetoric, however powerful, is not enough.
- Think systemic and big – policy alignment needs to be both horizontal and vertical.
- Realize that both local and central initiatives work – it is how leadership balances the two that is crucial.
- Focus on the building of local capacity and investing in leadership – appreciating that both are as important as a coherent national policy.
- Take an unrelenting focus on classroom practice – they see teachers as learners.
- Understand that reform does require additional resources – but the critical issue is how the resources are deployed.

With this as necessary background we now turn to a case study of educational reform in England. There are two reasons for including this detailed example. First, the English experiment with large-scale reform in primary schooling exhibits many of the characteristics, both positive and negative, that we have discussed so far. It is salutary, for example, to compare the English with the Ontario case, realizing of course that the Canadians deliberately built their own reform programme on the lessons learned from the pioneering work in England. The second reason for reviewing the English case is that it provides a paradigmatic example of the transition from large-scale to system-wide reform. As such, it provides evidence of the crucial policy conundrum which is the critical step in understanding the argument of how every school can become great.

The case of primary schooling in England

The determination of the British government to pursue education reform and bring about a step change in the performance of the education service is not in doubt. In its first term following the election in May 1997, the government sought, with passion and purpose, to turn into a reality Prime Minister Tony Blair's commitment to make 'education, education and education' his top three policy objectives. Following the June 2001 election at the start of the second term, Blair reaffirmed his commitment to the delivery of improved education within the context of a wider reform of the public services as a whole. Across the public services, the government pursued reform with some urgency, not least because it was clear that the public was impatient to see substantial evidence of progress on the ground.

Although the reform effort in England has involved both primary (elementary education for 5–11 year olds) and secondary schools (ages 11–16 or 11–18 for those schools with 'sixth forms') the focus of this section will reflect the performance of students within the 5–11 year age range during the first two terms of the New Labour government. The reason is simply because it is here where the link between reform strategy and student performance is most clearly seen.

England has since 1997 taken the opportunity to achieve high standards across an entire system of 24,000 schools and over 7 million school students. In order to move from the evidently underperforming system of the mid-1990s, the government put in place a policy approach best described as 'high challenge, high support'. The way in which these principles of 'high challenge, high support' are turned into practical policies to drive school improvement is summarized in Figure 2.1 (Barber 2001: 4).

The policies for each segment (starting at 12 o'clock) are set out in Table 2.1 (Barber 2001: 4). The important point is that the policy mix was complementary and mutually supportive.

Within the context of this large-scale long-term national reform effort the early focus on literacy and numeracy in primary schools was an important and

Figure 2.1 The high-challenge, high-support policy framework

Table 2.1 Complementary policies to drive school improvement

AMBITIOUS STANDARDS
- High standards set out in the National Curriculum
- National tests at ages 7, 11, 14, 16

DEVOLVED RESPONSIBILITY
- School as unit of accountability
- Devolution of resources and employment powers to schools

GOOD DATA/CLEAR TARGETS
- Individual pupil-level data collected nationally
- Statutory target setting at district and school level

ACCESS TO BEST PRACTICE AND QUALITY PROFESSIONAL DEVELOPMENT
- Universal professional development in national priorities (literacy, numeracy, ICT)
- Leadership development as an entitlement

ACCOUNTABILITY
- National inspection system for schools and LEAs
- Publication annually of school-district-level performance data and targets

INTERVENTION IN INVERSE PROPORTION TO SUCCESS
- School improvement grant to assist implementation of post-inspection action plan
- monitoring of performance by LEA (district)

necessary first step. Performance at age 11, at the end of Key Stage 2, is a key indicator. Competence in literacy and numeracy are absolutely vital to the life chances of children in our schools. They are the strongest predictors of success at age 16 and beyond. Yet despite this standards in primary schools had remained static since the historic Education Reform Act of 1944 irrespective of significant structural change that focused initially on centralization and, later, decentralization. As is seen in Figure 2.2 (Barber, in Brooks et al. 1996), it was only when the centralization/decentralization dichotomy was replaced by a system-wide commitment that standards began to rise.

The positive influence of the national literacy and numeracy strategies on student performance attracted worldwide attention. A graphic illustration of the impact that the strategies have had on the system as a whole is seen in the following series of maps. Figure 2.3 gives an indication of the number of local education authorities in England in 1998 where 75%+ of 11-year-old students were reading at their chronological age. This by itself provides sufficient justification for introducing the strategies (the map for numeracy was similar). The situation in 2002 is illustrated in Figure 2.4 and in 2004 in Figure 2.5. The picture for numeracy in 2002 and 2004 was also similar. Although there is still progress to be made the transformation of the national picture in six years is striking.

It is also important to realize that in terms of equity, the results have been sustained across the range of socioeconomic disadvantage. The analysis by 'free school meal band (FSM)' (which is the proxy measure for socioeconomic

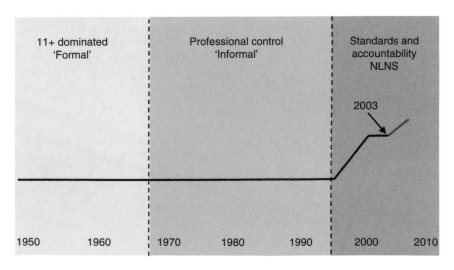

Figure 2.2   Brief history of standards in primary schools

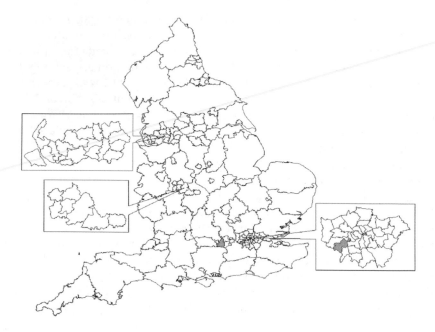

Figure 2.3 LEAs achieving 75%+ Level 4 English, 1998

Figure 2.4 LEAs achieving 75%+ Level 4 English, 2002

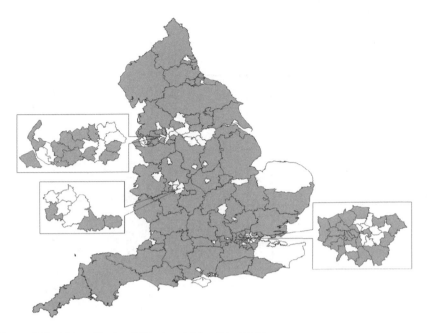

Figure 2.5   LEAs achieving 75%+ Level 4 English, 2004

disadvantage used in England) shows clearly that in every category students and schools are performing at the highest level and that the rise in the median level of improvement is consistent across free school meal bands (see Figure 2.6).

This level of progress was corroborated by the publication of the results of the Progress in International Reading Literacy (PIRLS) study. The PIRLS study is a comparative study of reading achievement of 10-year-olds in 2001 (Mullis et al. 2003). It is conducted under the auspices of the International Association for the Evaluation of Educational Achievement. Over 140,000 pupils in 35 countries participated in PIRLS 2001. Pupils in England scored more highly than those in the major European countries of France, Germany and Italy. They also scored significantly more highly than the other English-speaking countries in the survey: United States, New Zealand and Scotland. England was ranked third in terms of reading achievement with only Sweden and the Netherlands higher (see Figure 2.7, Mullis et al. 2003). This is in comparison to a similar study undertaken in the 1990s by the National Foundation for Educational Reserach (NFER), where England had a performance only around the international average, rather than the high position achieved in 2001.

The analysis of this success is however not entirely straightforward. The percentage increase in student performance in literacy and numeracy between 1997 and 2005 is illustrated in Table 2.2.

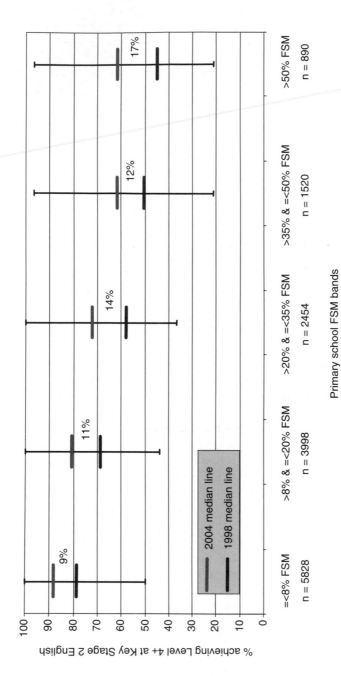

Figure 2.6 Percentage of pupils in mainstream schools achieving Level 4+ at Key Stage 2 English by primary school free school meal band, 2004, with 1998 median

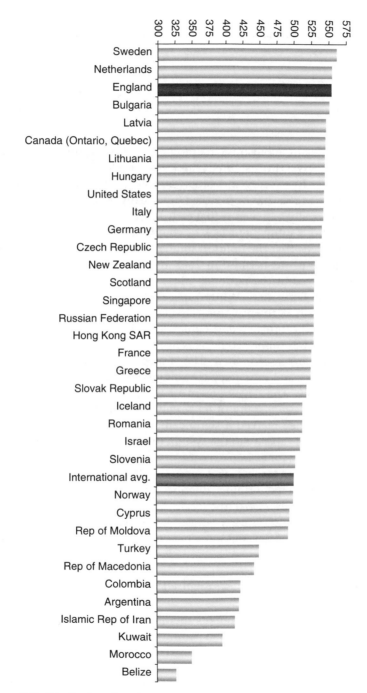

Figure 2.7 Distribution of reading achievement in 9–10-year-olds on PIRLS 2001

Table 2.2   Summary of Key Stage 2 results – percentage of pupils achieving Level 4+

	1997	1998	1999	2000	2001	2002	2003	2004	2005
English	63	65	71	75	75	75	75	77	79
Mathematics	62	59	69	72	71	73	73	74	75

What is significant about this data profile is that following an initial and significant increase over the first three years there was a levelling off in performance for the next three years and only recently has further progress been made. This is a trend that has been noted in virtually every large-scale reform initiative. What usually happens, is that early success is followed by a levelling off in progress and a subsequent lack of commitment to the programme of reform. I would argue that the uplift in standards in 2004 and 2005 following the four-year plateau was because in 2003 the national literacy and numeracy strategies merged into a national primary strategy as a consequence of the Excellence and Enjoyment White Paper (DfES 2003a), whose design was underpinned by many of the principles advocated in this book.

The focus on the broader curriculum and the learning experience of individual children was supported by a resolve to ensure that education policy was better aligned and coordinated. The strategy moved beyond the established role of literacy and numeracy consultants to support school improvement more generally. The development of the primary strategy leadership programme and the establishing of local networks for every primary school were crucial here. They marked a significant shift from the use of external expertise to the use of capacity in the system to lead change from within. The leadership programme, for example, is one of the largest initiatives of its kind; some 1800 serving head teachers were appointed and trained to work alongside colleagues in underperforming schools. In all, the programme impacted on 5,000 primary schools, 20% of the total.

In short the reform of primary education moved from a single focus on curriculum change in literacy and numeracy to a whole-school improvement effort that:

- had strong focus on personalized learning and assessment for learning
- re-orients materials to support the quality of teaching and learning and whole-school curriculum planning
- moves target setting from 'top down' to 'bottom up' with an increase in moderated teacher assessment
- provides clearer identification of and support for those schools and local authorities where progress was too slow

- contains a system-wide programme of leadership development and networking.

Let us now draw from this analysis a general lesson for large-scale/systemic reform. It is in the logic of large-scale reform that an early narrow focus on key skills produces an initial rapid increase in standards. To move beyond this plateau of achievement requires a system-wide school improvement approach that can deliver continuous improvement beyond the early gains. In other words, large-scale reform has characteristically focused on short-term objectives, whereas systemic change envisages a multi-phased process that ensures that early gains do not level off, but continue to improve as a consequence of employing strategies that at the same time raise achievement and build capacity.

From 'informed prescription' to 'informed professionalism'

It should be sufficiently clear from the narrative so far that the reform strategy in 1997 was unapologetically both top down and prescriptive. Michael Barber, its key architect, characterized the approach as 'informed prescription'. He compared this with what he described as the 'uninformed prescription' of the Thatcherite agenda that New Labour inherited. There is no doubt that 'informed prescription' was responsible for the impressive early gains and in the early stages of a long-term large-scale reform programme that 'informed prescription' has an important role to play. At least in England in the mid–late 1990s the system needed both energizing and the injection of knowledge that had the potential to change practice. In the medium term, however, informed prescription also has its downside and it may be this that accounts for the levelling off in performance after the initial increase in performance.

The real problem with 'informed prescription' is that teachers perceive the changes as imposed from outside and worry about the degree to which they can tailor and adapt the government's materials to their own purposes. There is also a concern that the changes, because of their external impetus, are not fully embedded or 'owned'. In this respect, the findings of the evaluation of the national literacy and numeracy strategies conducted by the Ontario Institute for Studies in Education, University of Toronto and University of Manitoba are instructive (Earl et al. 2003). On the positive side, they concluded that the strategies have influenced almost every primary classroom in England. The gap had narrowed substantially between pupil results in the most and least successful schools. Almost all schools received some training and teaching improved substantially since the strategies were first introduced. In particular, they noted improved coverage of literacy and numeracy, planning based on learning objectives rather than activities, more whole-class teaching and greater pace. There is still, however, considerable variation across teachers and schools in terms of subject knowledge, pedagogical skills and understanding, suggesting the need for greater capacity building than was originally envisaged.

The researchers concluded that in the early implementation of the strategies, pressure for compliance with central directives served to bring about large-scale change quickly. However, focusing on accountability for too long tends to create a culture of dependence and reduce professional autonomy. The responsibility for maintaining high standards and high-quality teaching needs to be embedded in the teachers, schools and Local Authorities to maintain and deepen early gains. There was an indication that giving teachers ownership of the strategies builds their capacity to adapt their teaching, solve problems and refine their practice while remaining true to the principles underlying the strategies. The researchers suggested that this is needed to establish long-term change and development.

Looked at in a broader public service reform perspective, in a fast-moving, large, complex system confidence, innovation and creativity at the frontline – where the service meets the customer – is of vital importance. Centrally driven policies, however good, cannot by definition deliver these vital characteristics. To achieve these outcomes some felt that the next phase of reform should signal a shift from what was called 'informed prescription' to a phase of what could be called 'informed professional judgement'.

Informed prescription does have the virtue of providing good ideas to a system that does not already have them. Its chief limitation is that it can never generate ownership and intrinsic motivation. And it may not be informed enough without the full creativity of teachers. Informed professional judgement has the potential of generating intrinsic motivation and good ideas, but it is only a 'potential'. To invest in professional judgement, when it is not well developed, represents a major political risk. In short, both prescription and judgement have their limitations.

This was the conundrum that policymakers in England faced as they contemplated the move from 'informed prescription' to 'informed professional judgement'. The key policy documents of the time acknowledged this dilemma and in theory proposed a way forward[7]. These policies offered heads

---

[7] The relevant government publications are:

DfES (2001b) White Paper *Schools Achieving Success*. London: Department for Education and Skills.

DfES (2002) *Investment for Reform*. London: Department for Education and Skills.

DfES (2003a) *Excellence and Enjoyment. A Strategy for Primary Schools*. London: Department for Education and Skills.

DfES (2003b) *Towards a Specialist System*. London: Department for Education and Skills.

DfES (2004c) *Five-year Strategy for Children and Learners*. London: Department for Education and Skills.

and teachers a new partnership, in which they, supported and encouraged by government, lead the next phase of reform. This, however, is within the context of an enabling but explicit policy direction focused on achieving systemic change. Bringing this about requires radical change in the way both government and teachers function. As Estelle Morris (2002), the then Secretary of State, argued in her foreword to the Schools Achieving Success White Paper: 'If we ask more of our teachers, we must also ask more of ourselves, and we must match our demands with more support.' This is no easy option for schools either, for the demand for continuous improvement comes from parents, government as well as the profession itself: being professionally autonomous is more challenging than being the recipient of benign policies.

This commitment is also seen in the phrase, the 'new relationship with schools', announced by David Miliband in his North of England speech in January 2004. In setting out his vision for personalized learning, he also argued that:

> *This will require a new relationship with schools which will give schools the time, support and information they need to focus on what really matters. By strengthening our school improvement process, improving our data flows and working with schools to tackle problems we will ensure there is a real focus on the central priorities of teaching and learning.*

Despite these good intentions, as New Labour moves into its third term it will be interesting to see how well it can manage the tension between 'prescription' and 'professionalism'. I believe that the jury is still out on this issue and that it reflects the two fundamental weaknesses in the approach to educational reform adopted by New Labour in 1997.

The first, which is a continuing theme of this book, is that the reform programme was not conceived within a long-term policy framework. Predictably and understandably, in the early heady years of a first-term reforming government, the question of how to sustain reform after early success had been achieved was not high on the agenda. More thought should have been given at the start of the reform process of how to build capacity for sustained improvement and how to manage the transition between national prescription and schools leading reform. In the terms used in the previous chapter, how over time to adjust the balance between 'outside – in' and 'inside – out' change. If this had been done at the outset, as in the case of Ontario, then I believe that the plateau effect, the perverse effects of top-down change and loss of momentum would all have been minimized.

Second, it is surprising that despite New Labour's commitment to the 'Third Way', that there was no overarching strategy for large-scale systemic educational reform. Of course there were flagship policies such as the National Literacy Strategy, Excellence in Cities and Academy programme, but these were essentially responses to presenting problems rather than a vision for the future of education. The signal failure of New Labour in its first two terms was its inability to develop a strategic and operational vision for public sector reform based on 'Third Way' principles. Anthony Giddens (1998) did an admirable job in laying the intellectual foundations for a Third Way political agenda, but neither he nor the politicians translated these into a distinctive programme of reform. As a consequence, New Labour has had great difficulty in reconciling in policy terms its longstanding commitment to social justice and its more recently acquired admiration for the power of market forces.

The next phase of reform must be driven by moral purpose, passion and a commitment to capacity building and the creation of new knowledge. It must also be recognized that this will require much more intensive and ongoing opportunities for teachers, heads and other staff in their schools to learn both individually and collectively drawing on their peers as well as on external experts and ideas. It is to a framework for considering this transition that we turn in the concluding section of this chapter.

The crucial policy conundrum and the four drivers for system reform

Let us now use this analysis of the English experiment with large-scale reform to frame the central question of the book. The argument goes something like this:

- Most agreed that standards were too low and too varied in the 1970s and 1980s and that some form of direct state intervention was necessary. The resultant 'national prescription' proved very successful particularly in raising standards in primary schools – progress confirmed by international comparisons.
- But as we have seen, progress plateaued in the second term and while a bit more improvement might be squeezed out nationally, and perhaps a lot more in underperforming schools, one has to question whether prescription still offers the recipe for sustained large-scale reform in the medium term.
- There is a growing recognition that schools need to lead the next phase of reform. But if the hypothesis is correct, and this is much contested terrain, it must categorically not be a naive return to the not-so-halcyon days of the 1970s when a thousand flowers bloomed and the educational life chances of too many of our children wilted.
- The implication is that we need a transition from an era of prescription

to an era of professionalism – in which the balance between national prescription and schools leading reform will change.

However, achieving this shift is not straightforward. As Michael Fullan (2003: 7) has said, it takes capacity to build capacity and if there is insufficient capacity to begin with it is folly to announce that a move to 'professionalism' provides the basis of a new approach. The key question is: 'How do we get there?' We cannot simply move from one era to the other without self-consciously building professional capacity throughout the system. It is this progression that is illustrated in Figure 2.8.

It is worth taking a little more time unpacking the thinking underlying the diagram. This is because it is fundamental to an understanding of the connection between 'every school a great school', systemic reform and system leadership, three of the key ideas crucial to the narrative of the book. I need to make five further points in order to elaborate the argument.

The first is to emphasize that this not an argument against 'top-down' change. As has already been stated neither 'top-down' nor 'bottom-up' change works just by itself; both have to be in balance – in creative tension. The balance between the two at any one time will, of course, depend on context.

Second, it must be realized that in England in 1997 it was clear that more central direction was needed. This reflects the balance towards national

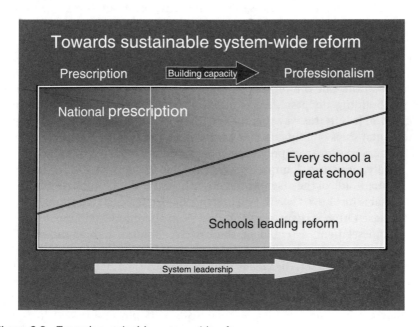

Figure 2.8 Towards sustainable system-wide reform

prescription as seen in the left-hand segment of the diagram. If we assume that time moves from left to right in the diagram, then, in the case of England, it is most probably correct to say that in terms of both policy and practice it is currently located in the middle segment of the diagram. This, as has already been seen, is contested terrain and there is no guarantee that there will be an inevitable movement into the right-hand segment.

Third, it should be no surprise to realize that the right-hand segment is relatively unknown territory. It implies horizontal and lateral ways of working with assumptions and governance arrangements very different from what we know now. The main difficulty in imagining this landscape is that the thinking of most people is constrained by their experiences within the power structure and norms of the left-hand segment of the diagram. Glimpses of the new landscape envisioned by the right-hand segment are scattered throughout the book.

The fourth point is both complex and critical. It is also difficult to phrase, as the literature of educational reform is contaminated with too much emotional and loose language. We bandy around phrases like 'radical reform' and words like 'transformation' without any attempt to define or reach a consensus on them and therefore we lose any collective sense of purpose. So, let me make my purpose here as clear as I can. The argument that I am making in this book is that for every school to be great requires a movement from left to right, with all that implies, in the terms of the central diagram of this chapter. The left to right movement is necessarily incremental as it builds on, rather than contradicts, the success of previous phases; yet, and this is the crucial point, the achievement of creating the educational landscape implied by the right-hand segment represents a step change from what has gone before. Yes, the difference between left- and right-hand segments represents a radical change or a transformation, but the process or journey from left to right will be incremental building on past success and reshaping in light of learning from experience. It is in this way that the language of school improvement (logical incremental steps building on past experience) and transformation (a qualitatively different state from previously) is reconciled.

Finally, of course, I am not suggesting that one always has to start from the left-hand side of the diagram and move in some sort of uniform way to the right. That is just how it was in England in 1997 for reasons that should now be crystal clear. Other systems may well start from the middle and move into the right-hand segment, as could be the case in Finland. Others may initially believe that they are in the right-hand segment. However, on further reflection it may be realized that if they really want to raise the standards for all students, then, as in the case of Ontario, a modified version of the English strategy that has a clear direction of travel from left to right may be the best place to start. If this diagram has any value it is as a heuristic – its purpose is to help people think rather than tell them what to do.

Coda: building capacity for system reform

I need to reiterate that the transition from 'prescription' to 'professionalism' is not straightforward. In order to move from one to the other, strategies are required that not only continue to raise standards but also build capacity within the system. This point is key: one cannot just drive to continue to raise standards in an instrumental way; one also needs to develop social, intellectual and organizational capital. Building capacity demands that we replace numerous central initiatives with a national consensus on a limited number of educational trends. There seems to me to be four key drivers that if pursued relentlessly and deeply have the potential to deliver 'every school a great school'. These are: personalized learning, professionalized teaching, networks and collaboration and intelligent accountability.

As seen in the 'diamond of reform' in Figure 2.9, the four trends coalesce and mould to context through the exercise of responsible system leadership. System leadership is therefore the most important driver; it also characterizes the dynamic in the right-hand segment of the diagram. As we shall see later, system leaders are those who care about and work for the success of other schools as well as their own.

Although this framework was developed from experience of working in the English context, I believe that it has global applicability. My experience of a number of developed and developing educational systems lead me to believe that these ideas resonate far beyond the boundaries of the English experience.

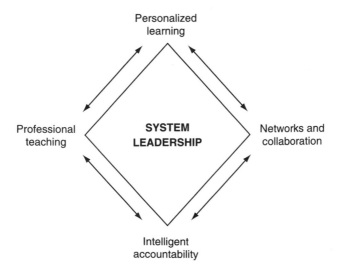

Figure 2.9   Four key drivers underpinning 'every school a great school'

For example, sitting in Beijing Normal University in October 2005, listening to the Deputy Minister of Education talk about her aspirations for the future of the Chinese educational system, convinced me that in education, as in many other aspects of life, the world is indeed becoming flat. Her eloquent and passionate discussion of personalization, assessment for learning, networking and self-evaluation was strikingly similar to the speeches we used to work on with Estelle Morris and David Miliband.

We have covered much territory in this chapter, but it has been necessary to set up the argument that for every school to become a great school, then large-scale reform efforts have to evolve into a systemic strategy. The four drivers of personalized learning, professionalized teaching, networks and collaboration and intelligent accountability provide the core strategy for systemic improvement. They are the canvas on which system leadership is exercised. Describing them in some detail and how they contribute to the building of a new lateral landscape for education provides the agenda for the next part of the book.

PART 2
The four drivers of system reform

In order to build capacity, while at the same time continuing to raise standards of achievement and learning, it is necessary that numerous national initiatives be replaced with a consensus on a limited number of educational trends. There are four key drivers that, if pursued relentlessly and deeply, have the potential to deliver 'every school a great school'.

3   Personalized learning

Personalized learning is an idea that is capturing the imagination of teachers, parents and young people around the world. It is an idea that has its roots in the best practices of the teaching profession and it has the potential to make every young person's learning experience stretching, creative, fun and successful.

Personalization is the guiding motif that allows a system to evolve from one based on delivery of services to one that emphasizes mass customization and co-production. It is about putting citizens at the heart of public services and enabling them to have a say in the design and improvement of the organizations that serve them. In education, this can be understood as personalized learning; the drive to tailor schooling to individual need, interest and aptitude. This emphasis provides a bridge from prescribed forms of teaching, learning skills, curriculum and assessment to an approach to classroom practice that is predicated on enabling every student to fulfil his potential.

In *Learning about Personalisation: How can We put the Learner at the Heart of the Education System?*, Charlie Leadbeater (2004: 6) clearly and sensitively links the concept of personalization with personalized learning as the key driver for the transformation of schooling. In terms of public sector reform Leadbeater argues that:

> *Public service reform should be user centred. It should be organised to deliver better solutions for the people who use the services. But it must also in the process, deliver better outcomes for society as a whole: effective collective provision to meet the need for education, health, transport, community safety and care for vulnerable people. The challenge is to build these two sources of value – for the individual users and the wider society – together. The combination creates public value.*

This approach according to Leadbeater (2004: 16) has the following consequences for education:

> *The foundation of a personalised education system would be to encourage children from an early age and across all backgrounds, to become more involved in making decisions about what they would like to learn and how. The more aware people are of what makes them learn, the more effective their learning is likely to be.*

He continues:

> *Personalised leaning does not apply market thinking to education. It is not designed to turn children and parents into consumers of education. The aim is to promote personal development through self realisation, self enhancement and self development. The child/learner should be seen as active, responsible and self motivated: a co-author of the script which determines how education is delivered.*

And:

> *The script of a system characterised by personalised learning . . . would start from the premise that the learner should be actively engaged in setting their own targets, devising their own learning plans and goals, choosing from a range of different ways to learn. . . . By making learning the guiding principle of the system, personalisation challenges some of the current divide and boundaries that exist – for example between formal and informal learning; between academic and vocational learning and between different ages and types of learners.*

In one sense, personalization represents a logical progression from the standards and accountability reform strategies of the 1990s. As we have already seen, these strategies marked an important first phase in a long-term large-scale reform effort. But in order to sustain system-wide improvement, societies are increasingly demanding strategies characterized by diversity, flexibility and choice.

In line with this, my view is that the genesis of personalization lies somewhere slightly different from the political emphasis with which it is currently associated. The foundations of personalization may be partly political, but mainly they reflect an ethical root.

It is moral purpose that drives personalization. We see it most vividly in the concern of the committed, conscientious teacher to match what is taught and how it is taught to the individual learner as a person. That is not just a question of 'sufficient challenge' of aligning pedagogy to the point of progression that each learner has reached, even though that is vitally important. It is also part of the teacher's concern to touch hearts as well as minds, to nourish a hunger for learning and help equip the learner with a proficiency and confidence to pursue understanding for themselves.

The concrete expression of the phrase 'every child is special' and the creation of an education system which treats them so, is what personalized learning is all about. That means overcoming the false dichotomies and the either/or which have bedevilled schooling for so long, so that for all pupils learning means both/and – both excellence and enjoyment, skills and enrichment, support and challenge, high standards and high equity, present success and long-term participation, deep engagement and broad horizons, and in so doing, breaking the link between socioeconomic disadvantage and attainment. That is the goal for personalized learning.

As David Miliband (2004), the Minister of State during the second term of New Labour said when he was introducing the concept of personalized learning into the English educational system:

> Giving every single child the chance to be the best they can be, whatever their talent or background, is not the betrayal of excellence; it is the fulfilment of it.

In exploring the concept of personalized learning in this chapter, I shall:

- define the concept a little further and review its main components
- explore the curricular implications of taking personalized learning seriously
- emphasize the metacognitive aspects of personalized learning
- in the coda, shall briefly discuss how to move personalized learning to scale.

What is personalized learning?

Personalized learning is not a new idea. Many schools and teachers have tailored curriculum and teaching methods to meet the needs of children and young people with great success for many years. What is new is the drive to make the best practices universal. It is re-imagining the education system around the learning needs and talents of young people that is the basis for every school becoming great.

David Miliband, again in his 2004 speech to the North of England Conference, described personalized learning as:

> [H]igh expectations of every child, given practical form by high-quality teaching based on a sound knowledge and understanding of each child's

needs. It is not individualized learning where pupils sit alone. Nor is it pupils left to their own devices – which too often reinforces low aspirations. It means shaping teaching around the way different youngsters learn; it means taking the care to nurture the unique talents of every pupil.

To build a successful system of personalized learning, we must begin by acknowledging that we should be giving every single child the chance to be the best she can be, whatever her talent or background. Personalized learning means high-quality teaching that is responsive to the different ways students achieve their best. There is a clear moral and educational case for pursuing this approach. A system that responds to individual pupils, by creating an education path that takes account of their needs, interests and aspirations, will not only generate excellence, it will also make a strong contribution to equity and social justice.

It is essential that personalized learning is not confused or conflated with individualized learning. The radical shift to what some consider the alternative to universalism – de-schooling options or an individualized or distance learning approach to teaching and learning at school age – would almost certainly set us back in terms of ensuring that every child gets a high-quality education. Individualized learning risks the weaker students most, for they are the ones who benefit from a well-structured learning environment. Individualized learning weakens the broader curriculum experience of the child, by reducing the social (and moral) dimension that is an inevitable part of learning together. In personalized learning, the input to the whole group is designed in a way that enables individual pupils to receive it differently according to their prior knowledge and experiences and the design of the learning process.

Education suffers as much as any aspect of public life from false dichotomies. The truth is that we need neither a mass system now nor an individualized system. We need a model that builds on a host of recent experiences and marches us confidently into an era when schooling is reliable and of high quality, while being much more accessible and more open to customization so that every child can get the education that he wants and needs. A mass service, which makes sense to every individual.

The nature of personalized learning can be portrayed by contrasting the alternatives of mass and individualised systems as seen in Table 3.1. The middle column in the table deliberately relates to personalized learning, demonstrating how it transcends and builds on the other two traditions.

One can summarize this approach to personalized learning as follows:

- As an educational aspiration, personalized learning reflects a system-wide commitment to moral purpose, high excellence and high equity and to every school being or becoming great.

Table 3.1 Contrasting personalized learning with mass provision and individualized education

Mass provision	Personalized learning	Individualized education
Teaching and learning takes place predominantly in the classroom	Teaching and learning constantly takes place in and beyond the classroom	Teaching and learning takes place predominantly out of the classroom and primarily at home
The teacher's role is to manage the class as well as to teach it	The teacher has all the classroom skills they need but works too within a school teaching-and-learning team which includes teaching assistants, tutors, mentors, counsellors and others to customize, enhance and extend children's work	The teacher is a tutor, a learning guide, a distance education-style mentor
Assessment for learning means the teacher keeps in view where the bulk of the class has got to, ready to move them to what's next	Assessment for learning means that every child's progress is monitored, so that customized support, remediation and enhancement can constantly be reappraised and put on offer	Assessment for learning means modules of works are distance marked, with the tutor sending recommendations of what to do next
The able child is ignored or denied	The able child gets opportunities for a special diet of extra extension and enhancement activities, with every effort made to spot them and to put them together where that's to their advantage	The able child can go at the pace they want, provided the materials available are suitably preprepared
The low attainer is ignored or denied	The low attainer gets the extra structure and support they particularly require	The low attainer is left to their own devices, just as much as the able child
A national curriculum that everyone follows can be highly specified	An NC framework remains – recommended areas of study – but can be slimmer and can be articulated at a deeper level (such as a learning	A national curriculum disappears and there's much more pupil choice of what to study and when/where

continued overleaf

Table 3.1   *(continued)*

Mass provision	Personalized learning	Individualized education
	journey), leaving much more scope for different children to work at different depths and for different periods of time	
The dominant pedagogy is that of the whole-class teacher	The pedagogy varies, fit for purpose, using the strengths of the best whole-class, group and individual work	The dominant pedagogy is that of ICT and the distant learning system
The curriculum experience gives access to social interaction and a strong moral framework that's essential to maintain social order within the bustling school	The curriculum experience continues to be social and moral – children and parents have to exercise more choice and are supported (and challenged) to take more responsibility for their educational choices	The curriculum experience is very light on social interaction and there's a risk of a weak moral educational side; the morals of the internet are more dominant
Parents mainly have responsibility for getting their children to and from school on time and do best not to interfere too much more	Parents share more responsibility as they take more part and help their children exercise more choice	Parents take responsibility for their children – or not.

- As an educational strategy, personalized learning relates to and builds on the learner's experience, knowledge and cognitive development, develops confidence and competence and leads towards autonomy, emancipation and self-actualization.
- As an approach to teaching and learning, personalized learning focuses on individual potential, develops the individual's learning skills (particularly ICT) and enhances creativity and social skills.
- As a curriculum orientation, personalized learning offers an approach to subject teaching that balances societal aspirations and personal relevance and unifies the curriculum offer across sectors and age groupings.

This leads directly to the following implications that can help guide day-to-day practices:

- *for children and young people*, it means clear learning pathways through the education system and the motivation to become independent, e-literate, fulfilled, lifelong learners
- *for schools*, it means a professional ethos that accepts and assumes every child comes to the classroom with a different knowledge base and skills set, as well as varying aptitudes and aspirations; and because of that, there is a determination for every young person's needs to be assessed and her talents developed through diverse teaching strategies
- *for school governors*, it means promoting high standards of educational achievement and well-being for every pupil, ensuring that all aspects of organizing and running the school work together to get the best for all pupils
- *for national and local authorities*, it means a responsibility to create the conditions in which teachers and schools have the flexibility and capability to personalize the learning experience of all their pupils; combined with a system of intelligent accountability so that central intervention is in inverse proportion to success
- *for the system as a whole*, it means the shared goals of high quality and high equity.

The rationale of these principles is clear: to raise standards by focusing teaching and learning on the aptitudes and interests of pupils and by removing any barriers to learning. The key question is how collectively we build this offer for every pupil and every parent.

Our starting point for delivering personalized learning is the expertise and professionalism of the whole school team. We know head teachers, teachers and support staff already do much to fulfil the potential of every pupil. Our belief is that there are six key components that can help to deepen and extend this personalization of education. Personalized learning occurs within an 'in and out' of school context where schools in a local community and beyond share both staff and curricular resources increasingly within a framework of shared accountability. Figure 3.1 illustrates the central components of personalized learning within and beyond the school.

This leads to an operational definition of personalized learning around six key components:

Assessment for learning
- self-directed learning
- powerful learning and teaching
- contribution of the 'new' technologies
- customizing the curriculum offer
- organizing the school and system for personalized learning.

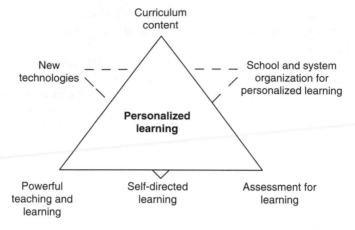

Figure 3.1 Central components of personalized learning within and beyond the school

Assessment for learning implies:

- That the school, its teachers and the system develop a high-level capacity for using data to promote student learning.
- The process of seeking and interpreting evidence for learners and teachers to decide where the learners are in their learning, where they need to go and how best to get there.
- Shared objectives, feedback that identifies targets for improvement, 'higher order' questioning and self- and peer assessment.

Self-directed learning implies:

- That self-directed learning contracts provide the basis for project work that is an essential and ongoing feature of the curriculum offer.
- Individual learning profiles.
- Counter-intuitivity – strong emphasis on cooperative group learning and social interaction.

Powerful learning and teaching implies:

- The curriculum should focus on understandings and competence that have enduring and intrinsic value.
- High expectations and challenging targets should be set for all, but while standards should remain constant, time and support should be varied according to individual student need.
- Teachers should show students how to incorporate new information into their existing knowledge through activities that induce critical thinking with conceptual problems.

The contribution of the 'new' technologies implies:

- Opportunity for personal creativity, the ability to match curriculum to individual learning styles and putting the pace of learning under the individual's control.
- Concurrent and extended learning opportunities outside of normal school day.
- Build diagnostic assessment for learning with different pathways to follow.

Customizing the curriculum offer implies:

- Modifying the framework of the National Curriculum to ensure a continuum for personalized learning across the three phases of education – foundation, middle and 14–19.
- Using the enquiry into subjects within the context of standards as the building block of curriculum provision.
- Involving students in the formulation of their own educational goals. This is the key to their establishing engagement in learning and establishing a long-term commitment to schooling.

Organizing schools for personalized learning implies:

- Differentiating the workforce for student learning, enhancing the role of the learning mentor and providing each learner with the link to an adult.
- Block timetabling and grouping students on basis of learning need, within and between schools to ensure network and community learning.
- Establishing a system of transferable learning profiles and credits to underpin assessment and to ensure flexibility.

Obviously, all of these six components are important as they intend to shape a modern pedagogy centred on learning, but they are not necessarily exclusive. Indeed, the approach adopted by the SSAT advocates nine gateways to personalizing learning (Hargreaves 2006). These are:

- student voice *and* assessment for learning
- learning to learn *and* the new technologies
- curriculum *and* advice and guidance
- mentoring and coaching *and* workforce development
- school design and organization.

I want here to highlight two aspects of personalization that are crucial to ensuring that every school becomes great. The first is 'customizing the curriculum offer' in order that breadth of study, personal relevance and flexible learning pathways can be delivered throughout the education system. The second is metacognition or 'learning how to learn'. Other aspects of the six components such as teaching and learning, the school organization and assessment for learning are addressed in subsequent chapters.

Towards the 'personalised' curriculum

It is the curriculum that provides the means for every school becoming a great school and every student realizing their potential. Yet in many educational systems the curriculum is often a barrier to achieving the forms of personalized learning so necessary for such a transformation. One way of both pinpointing the curriculum issue and of drawing the argument together is to pose the question: 'What does it mean to be educated' at any particular phase of education.

Being educated at any particular age has four central elements:

- a breadth of knowledge gained from a curricula entitlement
- a range of skills on a developmental continuum that reflects increasing depth at ages 7, 11, 14, 16, and in many cases, 18
- a range of learning experiences
- a set of key products, projects or artefacts.

It also means that students are sufficiently articulate to:

- sustain employability through basic skills
- apply their knowledge and skills in different contexts
- choose from and learn in a range of post–14 study (assuming an entitlement curriculum up until then)
- draw on wider experiences to inform further learning and choice.

I would suggest that most national curricula do not meet these desiderata. In general, central authorities set out mandatory programmes of study in all subjects, with schools generally free to determine their own timetables and design their own programmes of teaching. Although the following analysis was initially based on a reflection on the English KS3 (11–14) curriculum, the issues it raises and problems it identifies are intended to have a more general relevance. In particular, the following issues seem to be shared across many jurisdictions and militate against the realization of personalized learning:

- *Curriculum congestion.* The curriculum suffers from content and process overload. The consequence is congestion, with a breadth of study militating against students gaining a good grasp of knowledge and consolidated skills.
- *Expected levels.* Do clear levels of attainment exist in mother tongue, maths and science? Even if they do, is it certain that levels, or the way teachers interpret them, clearly test the functional application of literacy, numeracy and communication?
- *Poor catch-up provision or progression for low attaining pupils.* Too many schools do not build on what pupils have already learned. Schools frequently cite insufficient time in an overloaded curriculum for tailored catch-up provision as a key factor preventing their addressing low attainment, although teacher capacity is also a factor.
- *Inadequate embedding of core skills.* Schools have yet to fully embed teaching of literacy and numeracy across the curriculum.
- *Lack of clarity for students on the common learning skills.* Students often do not know what learning skills they should have acquired, in particular because skills are overly subject specific. Also, a combination of curriculum congestion and a lack of pedagogical expertise results in skills not being always effectively taught.
- *Insufficient stretch for the most able.* The pedagogy for identifying and developing giftedness is insufficiently embedded in classroom practice and assessment opportunities not taken up.
- *Staffing problems.* Lower secondary education in particular often suffers from a higher incidence of weak teachers, or frequent changes of staff, reflecting the priority given to teaching older students in both primary and secondary schools.

There is, of course, a spectrum of possible solutions for these problems. A general dilemma, however, is how to balance the need for change without the inevitable disruption caused by legislation to modify a statutory curriculum. The aim is always to achieve the maximum amount of reform while ensuring stability in the system. Although the following proposals are based on my understanding of the Key Stage 3 (11–14) curriculum in England, they represent a broader attempt to imagine a structure that enables schools and teachers to 'personalize' the curriculum across all stages of education.

The first is to *focus on core study*. Functional literacy, numeracy and communication could be clarified as expected attainment at the end of the KS3 curriculum. ICT would also need to be explicitly added to a suggested core of mother tongue, maths and science. Functional skills would similarly need to be embedded across the curriculum.

The second would be a *condensed statutory curriculum in non-core subjects combined with an optional entitlement.* In many countries, this is referred to as the 'essential curriculum'. This means that the statutory curriculum content and processes in non-core subjects would be reduced. As a rule of thumb in most national systems this would mean that the content removed would be approximately 20–25% of current specifications. The reduction could be re-designated as an optional entitlement. The entitlement would make up a number of components in the breadth of study currently set out for each subject. Schools would be required to teach a minimum number of components.

Third, the flexibility of an *optional entitlement* would allow schools to guarantee time to:

- secure essential knowledge and teach common learning skills through the curriculum
- organize the curriculum to meet the needs of a range of abilities, tailoring support for underachieving and underperforming students and to stretch gifted and talented students.

Fourth, there needs to be *clarity on common learning skills*. This requires that a common framework of skills is identified across the whole curriculum. As is seen in the following section this would include: enquiry; problem solving; creative thinking; information processing; reasoning; evaluation; communication. Students would develop each skill to a deeper level as they progressed through each stage of the curriculum. It is also necessary to look systematically across non-core subjects to consider how the spread and transmission of skills could best be improved to develop learning and raise attainment.

Finally, is the need to *champion effective pedagogy*. There needs to be external support to help schools organize the curriculum to meet the needs of a range of abilities. It must also help teachers bring curriculum knowledge and common learning skills together in the classroom.

The clear prize from pursuing these actions would be a curriculum tailored to the needs, talents and aptitudes of all students. This would ensure that every student had the core and common skills required to learn at each stage of education and that the best students were properly stretched.

In this section, I have taken a view on the necessary reform of any national or local curriculum to accommodate personalized learning. But underpinning the importance of structural curriculum change is the necessity that it accommodates not just curricular knowledge, but also 'learning how to learn'. To this essential aspect of personalized learning we now turn.

Metacognition and learning how to learn

Metacognitive skills enable students to develop the capacity to monitor, evaluate, control and change the way they think and learn. There is clear evidence that the acquisition of these skills can significantly increase achievement. To ensure more students gain these skills we need:

1   Teaching strategies that consistently and strategically develop students' learning skills. For example, instead of simply presenting information for knowledge acquisition, teachers can ensure that in tandem with learning new knowledge students also extract ideas, memorize information, build hypotheses and theories, use metaphors to think creatively and work effectively with others.

2   A framework of common learning skills, as there is currently a lack of clarity for students on the skills they should acquire and how they can develop these as they progress. These skills would need to be identified and taught coherently across the curriculum.

We will explore the first of these issues in the following chapter and a framework for learning skills in this. Inevitably, there is overlap between these two vital aspects of personalizing learning, as they are crucially the opposite sides of the same coin. Joyce et al. made this point in *Models of Learning – Tools for Teaching* (2002: 7), where we argued that it is the teacher's task not simply to 'teach', but to create powerful contexts for learning. It is a truism that no one can teach anyone anything: the best that can be done is to help another to learn. We expressed that idea and the essence of personalized learning in this way:

> *Learning experiences are composed of content, process and social climate. As teachers we create for and with our children opportunities to explore and build important areas of knowledge, develop powerful tools for learning, and live in humanising social conditions.*

It is the integration of 'content, process and social climate' that puts the 'power' into the personalized learning experience. Jerome Bruner has written evocatively about the dialectic between curriculum, teaching and learning. In his book, *Towards a Theory of Instruction* (1966: 21), he wrote:

> *Let me conclude with one last point. What I have said suggests that mental growth is in very considerable measure dependent upon growth from the outside in – a mastering of techniques that are embodied in the culture and that are passed on in a contingent dialogue by agents of the culture. . . . I suspect that much of growth starts out by our turning around on our own traces and recoding in new forms, with the aid of adult tutors, what we have been doing or seeing, then going on to new modes of organisation with the new products that have been formed by these recordings. . . . It is this that leads me to think that the heart of the educational process consists of*

providing aids and dialogues for translating experience into more powerful systems of notation and ordering. And it is for this reason that I think a theory of development must be linked to a theory or knowledge and to a theory of instruction, or be doomed to triviality.

There is a similarity, I think, between Bruner's notion of 'mental growth' and what is being referred to here as 'personalized learning'. Bruner argues convincingly for an integration of the ways in which individuals develop and grow, the ways in which they are taught and what it is that they are taught. Teaching is more than just presenting material; it is about infusing curriculum content with appropriate instructional strategies that are selected in order to achieve the learning goals the teacher has for her/his students. It is this 'holy trinity' of constructs that is of central relevance to the model of school improvement that was introduced in Chapter 1.

But at the heart of personalized learning is its impact, not just on test scores and examination results, but on the students' learning capability. If the teacher can teach the student how to learn at the same time as assisting them to acquire curriculum content, then the twin goals of learning and achievement can be met at the same time. There is now an increasingly sophisticated literature on how children learn (Wood 1998), the different types or 'multiple intelligences' (Gardner 1993a, 1993b) and the descriptions of a range of learning styles (Kolb 1984).

Although a discussion of these literatures is beyond the scope of this chapter, it is instructive to show how they have influenced the way in which we are defining personalized learning. One fundamental aspect of personalized learning is the ability of learners to respond successfully to the tasks that they are set, as well as the tasks they set themselves – in particular to:

- integrate prior and new knowledge
- acquire and use a range of learning skills
- solve problems individually and in groups
- think carefully about their successes and failures
- evaluate conflicting evidence and to think critically
- accept that learning involves uncertainty and difficulty.

The deployment of such a range of learning strategies is commonly termed metacognition, which can be regarded as the learner's ability to take control over his own learning processes. The key point is that within whatever context learning takes place, it involves an 'active construction of meaning'. This carries implications for the management of learning opportunities, in particular that an active construction of meaning requires practical, cognitive and other learning strategies. As learning is interactional it can occur only as the learner makes sense of particular experiences in particular contexts. This 'making sense' involves connecting with an individual's prior knowledge and experience. Thus, new learning has to relate to, and ultimately 'fit with', what individuals already understand.

This is where Vygotsky's (1962) insights extend, in my opinion, Bruner's (1960) tripartite integration of cognitive development, knowledge and teaching. His articulation of the 'zone of proximal development' has two key components.

The first relates to the necessity to focus instruction at that margin between what the learner already knows and what she/he can learn in the company of a more experienced or knowledgeable other, such as a teacher or a peer. Ensuring that teaching occurs within the learner's zone of proximal development is a 'meta-principle' for personalized learning. It is as relevant to the teaching of a class of 30 using classical interactive, but differentiated whole-class approaches, as it is to me when I am tutoring a doctoral student one to one during a supervision or when, in my other life, I am taking a group off-piste skiing in Chamonix.

The second aspect of Vygotsky's theory is not just identifying the learning zone but also discovering how to operate within the zone. It is here where the concept of 'scaffolding' is so powerful. 'Scaffolding' refers to the interactional support through dialogue, designed and led by the more competent other to maximize the child's learning, and to the gradual withdrawal of support as the child gains knowledge and competence. In the classroom, explanations, questions, recommended readings are commonly used as 'scaffolds'. Traditionally, researchers regarded 'scaffolding' as the guiding of a cooperative child, but more recent research has widened the concept by focusing on the children's active participation in problem solving.

This interactive view of learning is mirrored in the following chapter by a discussion of how a teaching strategy can also be a model of learning. But again I am getting ahead of myself. Having briefly discussed the process of learning we now have to give some attention to the skills of learning that need to be taught and acquired.

If we are serious about personalized learning, then, we need to be clear as to the typology of the skills students should gain in order to develop their personal effectiveness and employability. These skills fall into three categories:

- functional skills
- thinking and learning skills
- personal skills.

The argument so far has led us to a position where it is clear that:

- skills are a vital part of what it means to be educated

- there is currently:
  - insufficient clarity on the skills students should gain
  - no clear or coherent development of skills across most national curriculum
- the goal must therefore be to:
  - define a single framework of skills in which students should gain mastery across the curriculum
  - set out the ways in which these skills can best be delivered.

Having defined the three skills sets in which students should gain mastery it is worth looking in a little more detail as to what this framework entails.

Functional skills are literacy, numeracy and ICT. In most countries, these are regarded as key priorities and therefore tend to be taught and assessed in the core subjects of mother tongue, maths and ICT. We have already discussed how they can be integrated into a revised curriculum structure.

Thinking and learning skills are the skills young people need to acquire in order to become effective learners. Gaining mastery of these skills equips students to raise their achievement by developing their ability to:

- improve their achievement by applying a wide range of learning approaches in different subjects
- learn how to learn, with the capability to monitor, evaluate and change the ways in which they think and learn
- become independent learners, knowing how to generate their own ideas, acquire knowledge and transfer their learning to different contexts.

The specific thinking and learning skills[1] that I would suggest seem appropriate here are as follows:

Enquiry:
- ask relevant questions
- pose and define problems
- plan what to do and how to research
- monitoring progress in tackling a problem
- predict outcomes and anticipate consequences
- test conclusions, review solutions and improve ideas.

---

[1] These skills are based on the 'Thinking Skills' as set out in the National Curriculum Handbooks for Primary and Secondary teachers in England (DfEE/QCA, 1999a, 1999b). They also constitute part of the 'aspects of learning' as set out in the *Excellence and Enjoyment: Learning and Teaching in the Primary Years* materials developed by the Primary National Strategy (DfES 2004b).

Creative thinking:
- apply imagination to question and challenge ideas
- generate and extend ideas
- suggest hypotheses
- look for alternative innovative approaches and outcomes.

Information processing:
- locate and collect relevant information
- sort, classify, sequence, compare and contrast
- analyse relationships.

Reasoning:
- give reasons for opinions and actions
- draw inferences and make deductions
- use precise language to explain what they think
- make decisions informed by reasons or evidence.

Evaluation:
- assess evidence
- understand criteria for judging the value of own and others' work or ideas
- judge the value of what they read, hear and do
- have confidence in their judgements.

Personal skills are the skills young people need to acquire in order to develop their personal effectiveness. Gaining mastery of these skills equips students to manage themselves and to develop effective social and working relations. The specific skills that I suggest should comprise personal skills are as follows:[2]

Communication (and personal presentation):
- speak effectively for different audiences
- listen, understand and respond appropriately to others
- participate effectively in group discussions
- read fluently a range of literary and non-fiction texts and reflect critically
- write fluently for a range of purposes and audiences, including critical analysis of own and others' writing.

Diligence, reliability, and capability to improve:
- plan, organize and timetable effectively
- initiative and self-motivation

---

[2] The majority of these skills are currently set out as part of the 'Key Skills' and 'other aspects of learning' in the National Curriculum Handbooks for Primary and Secondary teachers in England (DfEE/QCA 1999a, 1999b).

- willingness to learn and progress
- reflect on own work and identifying ways to improve
- understand how decisions taken now can affect the future.

Working with others (social skills and teamwork):
- contribute to small-group and whole-class discussion and tasks
- work with others to meet a challenge: negotiate, resolve differences and support others
- social skills and awareness and understanding of others' needs
- leadership skills.

Moral and ethical awareness:
- spiritual: understand sense of self, strengths and weaknesses, unique potential, and will to achieve
- moral: understand difference between right and wrong, concern for others, consequences of actions and forgiveness
- social: understand responsibilities and rights of being a family and community members (local, national and global), how to relate to others and work for common good
- cultural: understand and respect own and other cultural traditions, appreciate and respond to a variety of experiences.

This framework provides clarity on the skills students should gain. But to ensure students gain mastery of these skills there needs to be agreement on how the skills should be:

1   embedded in teaching and learning, especially since in most systems these skills are not well taught in all schools and consequently students' skill development is patchy
2   developed coherently across the curriculum especially as again in most systems these skills are not specified or developed in a systematic way and progression is assumed rather than explicit.

In terms of functional skills, it would seem sensible that in most systems, as in England, literacy, numeracy and ICT should be (a) taught and assessed in the core subjects of English, maths and ICT and (b) have clear levels of progression written into national curriculum attainment targets and tests.

This means that thinking and learning skills, and personal skills, need to be accommodated. As thinking and learning skills and personal skills are cross-curricular (i.e. they transcend subject boundaries), they are therefore best acquired and developed through teaching and learning across the curriculum. In line with the argument in the following chapter, the most appropriate way of embedding these skills is through improved guidance and training in teaching and learning across the curriculum.

This has the great advantage that teachers become better skilled themselves in integrating the teaching and learning of skills into subject content. There are a variety of teaching and learning strategies that can be employed and these could be championed by a variety of national or locally based agencies. These include:

- subject-specific programmes that contribute to pupils' understanding, thinking and learning of key skills in a subject context
- discrete skills programmes (learning to learn lessons) that enable an explicit focus on skills with reference to a broad range of subject content and contexts
- cross-curricular programmes that ally clarity on learning skills with a focus on subject content to help students transfer their learning between lessons.

This skills framework is consistent with trends in other countries. For example, the OECD's (2005) Definition and Selection of Competencies (DeSeCo) Project, which classified individuals' key competencies for a successful life into three broad categories:

1   *Use tools interactively* (both physical and socio-cultural ones):
    - use language, symbols and texts interactively
    - use knowledge and information interactively
    - use technology interactively.

2   *Interacting in heterogeneous groups and specifically to*:
    - relate well to others
    - cooperate, work in teams
    - manage and resolve conflicts.

3   *Acting autonomously*:
    - act within the big picture
    - form and conduct life plans and personal projects
    - defend and assert rights, interests, limits and needs.

So, in summary, the clarity provided by a single skills framework allied with better guidance and training on pedagogy will itself create greater coherence across any national curriculum. This is the necessary foundation for ensuring that the essence of personalization is available for every student. This, in turn, is a critical building block in ensuring that every school is a great school. In the final section we examine further how these initiatives can be taken to scale.

Coda: moving personalized learning to scale

In this final section of the chapter, we discuss briefly how to move personalized learning to scale. In order for every school to be a great school, we cannot afford personalized learning to remain the achievement of just a few schools. At a minimum three complementary sets of activities are required to successfully move personalized learning to scale:

- First, the personalized learning offer needs to be developed and made the centrepiece of the range of national policy options. In parallel, curriculum content and subject specialism needs to be reviewed in light of the key components of personalized learning and relentlessly connected to the standards agenda. Table 3.2, for example, illustrates how this work was carried forward in England as part of the Key Stage 3 (lower secondary, 11–14 years old) national support programme.
- Second, the personal learning 'offer' needs to be the central agenda of all national and local partnership arrangements, e.g. national/local negotiations, the developing of a consensus among national support organizations, mobilizing non-governmental organizations.

Table 3.2 Key Stage 3 and personalized learning

Assessment for learning	• Setting personal pupil targets • Introducing self- and peer assessment • Developing more effective feedback to pupils
Self-directed learning	• Teaching study and research skills • Introducing learning contracts
Powerful learning and teaching	• Developing thinking and learning skills across the curriculum • The learning challenge programme • Mentoring skills
Contribution of the 'new' technologies	• Implementing ICT across the curriculum • Teaching the use of the internet • Interactive teaching programmes
Customizing the curriculum offer	• Guidance on different curriculum models for KS3 • The 2-year KS3 pilot – creating time for the tailored curriculum
Organizing the school and system for personalized learning	• Models and materials for catch-up provision • Involving parents project • Teaching strategies that include and challenge everyone

Table 3.3 A matrix for reflecting on the potential of personalized learning at various levels in the system

PERSONALIZED LEARNING	Learning classrooms	Learning schools	Learning systems
Assessment for learning	Appreciation of pupil involvement in goal setting and learning from feedback	Enquiry-led and data-driven school improvement	National system for credit transfer, pupil-learning profiles and learning vouchers
Self-directed learning	Personalized learning strategies and skills with personal learning support, proportionate to need	Professional learning communities	Innovation, knowledge sharing and network learning at all levels and across the system
Powerful learning and teaching	Self-directed learning contracts and projects	Project-based work and curriculum options shared between schools and in community	National assessment based, in part, on student projects during each course of study as part of final assessments
Contribution of the 'new' technologies	Enquiry into subjects through project-based work	Scope for different students to work at different depths for different periods of time	National Curriculum based on personalized learning principles and links through KS 1, 2, 3 and 14–19
Customizing the curriculum offer	Repertoire of ICT teaching strategies and awareness of different learning styles	ICT learning opportunities between schools and in community	National Grid for Learning extended to accommodate personalized learning
Organizing the school and system for personalized learning	Subject focus (content), methodological range (process) and environment for learning	School-specific whole-school approach with tailored external challenge and support	Establishing networks with emphasis on diversity, collaboration, innovation, lateral accountability and trust

- Third, personalized learning and moral purpose must be made synonymous, i.e. personalized learning is important because it will enable all young people to reach their potential. Personalized learning becomes the key message in national and local government's communication policy and conferences, as well as the recipient of a series of symbolic (and substantive) policy initiatives, e.g. learning vouchers for every 14 year old.

To meet the full range of individual needs and aspirations inherent in the goal of excellence for all requires extensive, but disciplined innovation of many different kinds and at different levels in educational provision and professional practices (see Table 3.3). This entails changes at *classroom level*, for example through ICT training for classroom teachers and leaders to build on the ICT infrastructure; at *school level*, for example through workforce reform to ensure that teachers spend more time actually teaching; and at *system level*, for example through the creation of federations between schools and other collaborative arrangements. It should by now be clear that the dissemination of the outcomes of innovation and new methods of achieving excellence cannot be achieved by a centre-periphery model alone, but require new mechanisms of lateral transfer through networks as discussed in Chapter 6.

The challenge for personalized learning is to create a *learning system* that is capable of adapting to deep changes in our economy and society by pursuing universal participation and achievement. In the following chapter, we explore the implications such an approach to learning has on our concepts of teacher professionalism.

4   Professionalized teaching

It is clear that personalized learning requires a radical readjustment to the way in which teachers teach and schools organize themselves. Teachers need to move to a new phase of professionalism, where they are increasingly focused on and accountable for the way in which they use data and evidence to apply a rich repertoire of pedagogic strategies to personalize learning for all of their students. Unfortunately, this approach to teaching is still not commonplace and achieving this level of professionalism seems to be a continuing challenge.

It is an issue that reaches to the heart of what it means to teach and be a teacher in a school. As was discussed in the introduction, it is about developing a 'practice' of education. Richard Elmore (1995b: 366) explains the problem in this way:

> *Principles of [best] practice [related to teaching and learning] . . . have difficulty taking root in schools for essentially two reasons: (a) they require content knowledge and pedagogical skill that few teachers presently have, and (b) they challenge certain basic patterns in the organisation of schooling. Neither problem can be solved independently of the other, nor is teaching practice likely to change in the absence of solutions that operate simultaneously on both fronts.*

The problem is in fact twofold. First, the depth of professional skill required for personalizing learning is not evident among most teachers; and, second, even if it were, without a flourishing professional development culture within the school best practice would not become commonplace. Without its becoming pervasive there is no whole-school effect, no high expectations, no innovation and no consistency of practice. Personalized learning in such schools is nothing but an illusion.

As we strive for every school to be a great school, it is the continuing professional development of teachers (CPD) that is at the heart of the response.

Put simply, unless teachers see their continuing development as an essential part of their professionalism, the system will be unable to make the next big step forward in standards of learning and achievement. This is not just an 'academic' issue about making teaching more comparable to other great modern professions, but it is a highly practical, standards-based issue about how we deliver personalized learning and fulfil the potential of every student. To address this, teachers need continually to be learning from each other, developing knowledge in their subject area and in pedagogy, and using rich data on pupil progress to individualize teaching styles and strategies. Moreover, schools and teachers need to be seizing this agenda and seeing CPD as a responsibility that extends beyond the strict confines of the school day.

However, and in building on Elmore's critique, there are two major impediments in sustaining such an approach to teacher professionalism:

1   We simply do not have a sufficiently robust and sophisticated language in this country for talking about teaching. If teachers had a more extensive vocabulary of professional practice, they could exercise more control over the learning environments of their students and their own professional development. This implies an ability to use a range of whole-class, group and individual teaching, learning and ICT strategies to transmit knowledge, to instil key learning skills and to accommodate different paces of learning. A key task for those committed to enhancing the more personalized learning of pupils, therefore, is to expand the vocabulary of teaching.

2   Available evidence on the effectiveness of the average professional development initiative is far from encouraging.[1] Despite all the effort and resources that have been utilized, the impact of such programmes in terms of improvements in teaching and better learning outcomes for pupils is rather disappointing. The research provides a bleak picture of in-service initiatives that are poorly conceptualized, insensitive to the concerns of individual participants and, perhaps critically, make little effort to help participants relate their learning experiences to their usual workplace conditions. In order to maximize teacher effect on learning, we need to ensure that professional development directly impacts on teacher behaviour. This demands opportunities for teachers to engage newly learnt skills in the workplace through immediate and sustained practice, collaboration and peer coaching and studying development and implementation.

[1] See for example Fullan, M. (2001) *The New Meaning of Educational Change*, 3rd edn. New York: Teachers' College Press.

To summarize, in order to deliver personalized learning: first, a minimum of three conditions need to be in place: teachers need to be competent in the way they use data, evidence and formative assessment; they need a range of teaching strategies to respond to the diversity of their students' learning needs; this, in turn, implies radically different forms of professional development with a strong focus on coaching and establishing schools as professional learning communities. The first of these issues, formative assessment, is discussed in the following chapter, the last two concerns provide the substance of the discussion that follows. In elaborating on them, I will:

- first, offer a framework in which to think about teaching
- second, describe some examples of the 'models of teaching' approach that is critical in linking teaching strategy to learning skill
- then review the approaches to professional development that ensure impact on classroom practice
- finally, I say a few words in the coda about moving professional development to scale.

A framework for thinking about teaching

In *School Improvement for Real* (Hopkins 2001: Chapter 5), I introduced a framework for thinking about teaching and learning. I briefly refer to it again here, as it still seems to me to provide a useful starting point in the quest to develop a language and practice for teaching. Figure 4.1 illustrates the four elements of the framework that interestingly are often regarded as being contradictory rather than complementary. Let us look at each of them in turn.

I start with teaching skills because these are the basic building blocks of teacher competence. These are the everyday classroom management skills that most teachers became familiar with during their initial training and that they continue to refine as part of their reflection on professional practice. These are behaviours such as: content coverage, engaged time (i.e. students learn more when they are on task for a high proportion of class time), active teaching, structuring information, wait time and effective questioning. There is an extensive research literature on teaching effects that are replete with cues and tactics necessary for effective teaching. Consistently high correlations are achieved between student achievement scores and classroom processes.[2] The research evidence on those teaching behaviours most closely

---

[2] See Brophy, J. and Good. T, (1986) Teacher behaviour and student achievement in Wittrock, M. (ed.) *Handbook of Research on Teaching*, 3rd edn. New York: Macmillan; and Brophy, J. (1983) Classroom organisation and management, *The Elementary School Journal*, 82 (4): 266–85.

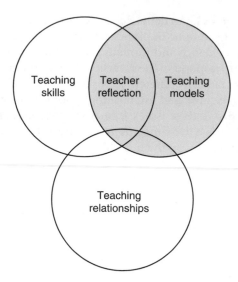

Figure 4.1 Four ways of thinking about teaching

associated with student achievement gains is now very sophisticated. An excellent summary is provided by Bert Creemers (1994: 88) in his book *The Effective Classroom*. They are taken from his 'basic model of educational effectiveness' that sees the quality of instruction as having three main components, viz. curriculum, grouping procedures and teacher behaviour. These are all, of course, essential aspects of the skills sets teachers need in order to personalize learning. The characteristics of teacher behaviour seen in Table 4.1 (Creemers 1994) all have strong empirical support in the research literature.

The second component is what I have called teaching relationships. These are less technical and are more related to the teacher's commitment to her/his students and belief in the power of high expectations. A supportive, rigorous and optimistic learning environment is fundamental for high levels of student achievement. For me, a key aspect of teaching is the teacher's ability to generate and sustain an authentic relationship with her students. For example, the teacher 'who made a difference' is a common topic of conversation following one's admission that 'I am a teacher'. To many educators a prime indicator of the 'effective' school is one in which high proportion of pupils 'have a good or "vital" relationship with one or more teachers'.

The influence of expectations is often a subtle one and is felt within myriad classroom interactions. The ways in which the teacher sets tasks, arranges groups, locates the responsibility for learning and provides feedback, are all illustrations of how teachers can give messages of high expectations and support that condition and enhance student behaviour. It implies establishing the classroom as a safe and secure learning environment in which pupils can

Table 4.1   Characteristics of teacher behaviour associated with student achievement gains

- **Management of the classroom** to create a situation where learning can take place. This implies an orderly and quiet atmosphere in the classroom, although learning itself requires more than a well-organized class. Moreover, effective teaching itself contributes to the management of the class

- **Provision of homework.** If properly organized, homework contributes to effectiveness. This implies a clear structure of assignments and provision and evaluation of homework

- **Expectations** teachers (and schools) have of their abilities to influence student outcomes probably influence what teachers do. We can expect those expectations to become apparent in the actual teacher behaviours

- **Clear goal setting.** This includes a restricted set of goals and an emphasis on basic skills and on cognitive learning and transfer. The content should be chosen in line with these goals

- **Structuring the content.** This includes the ordering of the content according to hierarchy-ordered goals. The use of advanced organizers can also structure the content for students. The use of prior knowledge can increase students' own contributions and responsiveness for learning

- **Clarity of presentation,** which implies the elements mentioned already but also refers to the transfer process itself (avoiding vagueness and incomplete sentences)

- **Questioning** (by means of low- and higher order questions) keeps students at work and can be used to check their understanding

- **Immediate exercise after presentation.** Like questioning, exercises provide a check for understanding and can be used to clarify problems

- **Evaluating** whether the goals are obtained, by means of testing, providing feedback and corrective instruction

expect acceptance, respect and even warmth from their teachers, without having to earn these – they are intrinsic rights that are extended to all pupils, without prejudice, simply because they are there.

I had a somewhat paradoxical example of this recently when I was in a school in Antofagasta, a mining town in the north of Chile. The school was new, built by the local mining company and situated right next to a *favela*. It was one of the most deprived shanty towns I have ever seen. During the visit the head took me aside and said animatedly: 'Do you know, David, the best tool we have for helping these children is not our brain but our heart.' He was a kind man and I knew what he meant. But I only half agreed with him. Of course, those children needed love and support and acceptance, but they also needed the knowledge and skills to enable them to escape from the *favela*, to transcend their context and not to be imprisoned within it. Teaching relationships in the way I am describing here embodies both and is at the very core of personalized learning.

These two perspectives on high-quality teaching are not discrete. It is the practice of fine teachers to combine these elements through a *process of reflection* to create an individual style. Consequently, it may be that critical systematic reflection is a necessary condition for quality teaching. This is not reflection for reflection's sake, but in order to continue to develop a mastery of one's chosen craft. It is through reflection that the teacher harmonizes, integrates and transcends the necessary classroom management skills and the personal aspects of her/his teaching into a strategy that has meaning for her/his students.

In my experience, it is these three elements well integrated into a distinctive individual approach that most people would regard as being the definition of a good, indeed very good, teacher. In England, for example, such a teacher would be highly regarded both by external inspectors and her/his peers. But for me this is a necessary, but not a sufficient condition for the quality of teaching required to personalize learning. As we saw in the previous chapter personalized learning is about developing learning capability and involving students in creating their own meaning and learning pathways. In some ways, and perhaps this is a little unfair, the approach to teaching I have just described could be regarded as just a refinement, albeit a sophisticated one, of the traditional 'transmission' or 'recitation' approach to teaching. This method is in stark contrast to the approach to teaching envisioned by advocates of personalized learning, where the teacher is cast in an entirely different role – that of a creator of increasingly powerful learning experiences. It is this approach to teaching that provides the fourth element in the framework – *teaching models*.

In the previous chapter I made the point, as I have just done above, that it is the teacher's task not simply to 'teach', but to create powerful contexts for learning. I then quoted from our book *Models of Learning – Tools for Teaching* (Joyce et al. 2002: 7):

> *Learning experiences are composed of content, process and social climate. As teachers we create for and with our children opportunities to explore and build important areas of knowledge, develop powerful tools for learning, and live in humanising social conditions.*

Let me now complete the quotation (Joyce et al. 2002: 7), in support of the argument that a good teaching strategy can also be a powerful learning strategy:

> *Our toolbox is the models of teaching, actually models for learning that*

> *simultaneously define the nature of the content, the learning strategies, and the arrangements for social interaction that create the learning environments of our students.*
>
> *Through the selection of appropriate models, content can become conceptual rather than particular, the process can become constructive inquiry instead of passive reception and the social climate can become expansive not restrictive. Our choices depend on the range of our active teaching repertoire and our efforts to expand it by developing new models and studying those developed by others.*

It is the integration of 'content, process and social climate' that explains how the learning experience can be organized and personalized to make a positive difference to students. The impact is not just on test scores and examination results, but also on the students' capacity to learn. This is the heart of the matter. If the teacher can teach the student how to learn at the same time as assisting them to acquire curriculum content, then the twin goals of learning and achievement can be met at the same time.

Thus, imagine a classroom where the learning environment contains a variety of models of teaching that are not only intended to accomplish a range of curriculum goals, but are also designed to help students increase their competence as learners. At the risk of gilding the lily, allow me one final quote from *Models of Learning – Tools for Teaching* (2002):

> *In such classrooms the students learn models for memorising information, how to attain concepts and how to invent them. They practise building hypotheses and theories and use the tools of science to test them. They learn how to extract information and ideas from lectures and presentations, how to study social issues and how to analyse their own social values. These students also know how to profit from training and how to train themselves in athletics, performing arts, mathematics and social skills. They know how to make their writing and problem solving more lucid and creative. Perhaps most importantly, they know how to take initiative in planning personal study, and they know how to work with others to initiate and carry out co-operative tasks. As students' master information and skills, the result of each learning experience is not only the content they learn but also the greater ability they acquire to approach future learning tasks with confidence and to create increasingly effective learning environments for themselves.*

Bruce Joyce developed this approach with his colleagues in his pioneering work *Models of Teaching*, which was first published in 1972 and is now in its seventh edition. Joyce describes and analyses over 30 different models of teaching – each with its own 'syntax', phases and guidelines – that are designed to bring about particular kinds of learning and to help students become more effective learners.

The models of teaching are therefore tools that teachers can use to create increasingly personalized learning experiences. But such research and strategies should not be regarded as panaceas to be followed slavishly. Research knowledge and the various specifications of teaching can have limitations, especially if they are adopted uncritically. Such knowledge only becomes useful when it is subjected to the discipline of practice through the exercise of the teacher's professional judgement. For, as Lawrence Stenhouse (1975) once argued, such proposals are not to be regarded 'as an unqualified recommendation, but rather as a provisional specification claiming no more than to be worth putting to the test of practice. Such proposals claim to be intelligent rather than correct'. It is in this way that the use of 'teaching models' form part of an overall strategy for enhancing teacher professionalism.

Models of learning – tools for teaching

Models of teaching simultaneously define the nature of the content, the learning strategies and the arrangements for social interaction that create the learning environments of students. Models of teaching are also models of learning. How teaching is conducted has a large impact on students' abilities to educate themselves. Each model has its own core purpose that relates not only to how to organize teaching, but also to ways of learning. So, for example, if in whole-class teaching the teacher uses the advance organizer model to structure a presentation, the student can use the same method as a means of extracting information and ideas from lectures and presentations.

Some examples of the relationship between teaching and learning strategy are given in Table 4.2.

Table 4.2 Examples of the relationship between model of teaching and learning skills

Model of teaching	Learning skill
Advanced organizer (or whole-class teaching model)	Extracting information and ideas from lectures and presentations
Groupwork	Working effectively with others to initiate and carry out cooperative tasks
Inductive teaching	Building hypotheses and theories through classification
Mnemonics	Memorizing information
Concept attainment	Attaining concepts and how to invent them
Synectics	Using metaphors to think creatively

It is important to be clear about what is meant by a 'model of teaching'. As the idea is exotic to the repertoires of many teachers, one needs to be quite concrete in explaining the concept. This is what I will attempt to do in this section. An initial distinction would be to regard the evidence on teaching skills as providing the teacher with tactical knowledge, whereas the research on 'models of teaching' gives teachers strategic knowledge about how to create whole classroom settings to facilitate learning.

In *Models of Learning – Tools for Teaching* (2002) and the *Creating the Conditions for Teaching and Learning* (Hopkins et al. 2000) handbook which was based on experiences in IQEA schools, a range of contrasting and complementary teaching strategies are described. These are drawn from Joyce's original four families of teaching model, namely the information processing, the social, the personal, and the behavioural families. Here are brief descriptions of three of the models of teaching and learning, followed by a more curriculum-focused example.

The whole-class teaching model [3]

In active whole-class teaching the teacher controls pupils' learning and seeks to improve performance through direct instruction, whole-class questioning, discussion and learning activities. It is the most common model of teaching on the planet, yet common practice rarely follows the syntax of the model as described here.

This model of teaching enables pupils to order, absorb, understand and relate different areas of knowledge efficiently. It is not a matter of instruction alone. As well as enabling students to process information, the model also allows for pupil interaction so that they learn from each other as well as the teacher and extend their repertoire of social skills.

The model presupposes a coherent teaching programme based on a clear set of overarching goals, but it is not inclusive to these goals. It works as part of an integrative teaching and learning plan that may include cooperative groupwork and independent study. Employing a range of teaching activities influences pupil motivation and is likely to engage them in learning.

It is important to emphasize that whole-class teaching is a strategic approach to teaching that not only focuses on basic skills and cognitive processes, but also on promoting learning strategies, problem solving and social support. Teachers using the whole-class model address these more complex instructional goals by using a range of techniques to structure strategic

---

[3] Adapted from Chapter 5 in Hopkins. D., Harris, A., Singleton, C. and Watts, R. (2000) *Creating the Conditions for Teaching and Learning. A Handbook of Staff Development Activities*. London: David Fulton.

learning. A number of these teaching behaviours have already been identified in Table 4.1.

In summary, the whole-class model of teaching includes the following five phases:

1   *Review*:
    • Review the concepts and skills from the previous lesson (and if appropriate the homework).
2   *Presenting information*:
    • Lecture or talk:
        • Preview the outline and scope of the lecture.
        • Introduce key terms or concepts.
        • Lecture proceeds in small steps, starting with what is familiar and using lively explanations and illustrations.
    • Demonstration:
        • Preliminaries – a guide as to what to observe and expect.
        • Preview – purpose is outlined.
        • Rehearsal – teachers go through each step.
        • Reprise – procedures are repeated.
3   *Involving pupils in discussion*:
    • Focus on meaning and promoting student understanding through fast-paced discussion.
    • Assess student comprehension through high-quality questioning.
4   *Engaging pupils in learning activities*:
    • Design activities to focus on content.
    • Implementation of learning activities.
5   *Summary and review*:
    • Pupils ask follow-up questions, share findings and conclusions.
    • Teacher reinforces key points, emphasizes central ideas and sums up achievements.

The cooperative groupwork teaching model

As a model of teaching cooperative groupwork has a powerful effect in raising pupil achievement because it harnesses the synergy of collective action. It combines the dynamics of democratic processes with the processes of academic enquiry. It encourages active participation in learning and collaborative behaviour by developing social as well as 'academic' skills. Thus, the model requires pupils to practise and refine their negotiating, organizing and communication skills, define issues and problems, develop ways of solving them including collecting and interpreting evidence, hypothesizing, testing and re-evaluating.

The model is highly flexible and draws on a wide range of methods – individual research, collaborative enquiry and plenary activities – and allows the integration of them all into a powerful teaching tool. The teacher is able to conduct a more subtle and complex learning strategy that achieves a number of learning goals simultaneously. Thus, styles can vary from didactic to 'light touch' teaching where teacher is more an adviser and guide than a director. Examples of cooperative group activities are: numbered heads, jigsaw, twos to fours or snowballing, rainbow groups, envoys, listening triads and critical friends.

Space precludes a discussion of all these, but it is worth describing a little more detail one of them to give a flavour of the model. A popular approach to cooperative group learning is the 'jigsaw'.

Stages for jigsaw groups (Hopkins 2002b: 111):

1   Teacher sets up the content of the inquiry, i.e. engages the pupils' minds in an enquiry to be 'solved'.
2   Teacher puts pupils into equal-sized groups if possible – called the home groups. Teacher gives each group an identical brief with each group member having different job/roles. The pupils discuss the enquiry and allocate jobs/roles for a short time. Each pupil needs to be clear what their job involves.
3   The home groups divide – all pupils now join those who have identical jobs – the expert groups. Pupils have to gather information/form opinion, etc. The information is usually provided by the teacher or texts. This could take time, according to the tasks set.
4   Pupils reassemble in the home groups and, armed with different information, collate their ideas to do the following:
    • solve the enquiry
    • debate the issue.
5   Overall feedback to the whole class may not be necessary. If it is, many forms of feedback can be used, e.g.:
    • go round the groups asking people with different roles to report back in each group (i.e. the groups have no choice about who is their reporter)
    • 'quick' posters displayed around the room and the class go round to compare
    • whole-class discussion in a circle
    • individual writing up about the whole group topic, etc.

There are a wide range of strategies that comprise the cooperative group work teaching model, underpinned by the following principles (Johnson et al. 1993):

- *Positive interdependence*. When all members of a group feel connected to each other in the accomplishment of a common goal. All individuals must succeed for the group to succeed.
- *Individual accountability*. Holding every member of the group responsible to demonstrate the accomplishment of the learning.
- *Face-to-face interaction*. When group members are close in proximity to each other and enter into a dialogue with each other in ways that promote continued progress.
- *Social skills*. Human interaction skills that enable groups to function effectively (e.g. taking turns, encouraging, listening, giving help, clarifying, checking, understanding, probing). Such skills enhance communication, trust, leadership, decision making and conflict management.
- *Processing*. When group members assess their collaborative efforts and target improvements.

The inductive teaching model

Inductive teaching encourages pupils to build, test and use categories to organize their thinking about a particular topic or subject area through classification.

The inductive method allows pupils to understand a variety of classifications in a structured way that includes a variety of teaching techniques within one method. The opportunity for reclassification or hypothesizing, enhances learning potential and develops high-order thinking. The inductive model of teaching consists of a number of discrete phases as now seen. These cannot be rushed or omitted. Inductive inquiries are rarely brief because the very nature of the inquiry requires pupils to think deeply. The key activity in the inductive model is the collecting and sifting of information in order to construct categories or labels. This process requires pupils to engage with the data and seek to produce categories in which to allocate the data. It requires them to generate hypotheses based on this allocation and to test out these hypotheses by using them to guide subsequent work.

In summary, the inductive model of teaching involves the following six phases (Joyce and Calhoun 1998):

Phase One: identify the domain:
- Establish the focus and boundaries of the initial inquiry.
- Clarify the long-term objectives.

Phase Two: collect, present and enumerate data:
- Assemble and present the initial dataset.
- Enumerate and label the items of data.

Phase Three: examine data:
- Thoroughly study the items in the dataset and identify their attributes.

Phase Four: form concepts by classifying:
- Classify the items in the dataset and share the results.
- Add data to the set.
- Reclassification occurs, possibly many times.

Phase Five: generate and test hypotheses:
- Examine the implications of differences between categories.
- Classify categories, as appropriate.
- Reclassify in two-way matrices, as well as by correlations, as appropriate.

Phase Six: consolidate and transfer:
- Search for additional items of data in resource material.
- Synthesize by writing about the domain, using the categories.
- Convert categories into skills.
- Test and consolidate skills through practice and application.

I have concentrated on the 'models of teaching' approach for reasons of familiarity. There are, however, many other teaching strategies that impact powerfully on a student's capacity to learn, such as the cognitive acceleration through science education (CASE) for example. CASE is a curriculum and teaching project based at King's College in London that has reported some striking long-term effects on secondary children's academic achievement. The researchers, Philip Adey and Michael Shayer, claim successful intervention for between 25% and 50% of children taught using CASE teaching strategies. Results in 1994, 1996 and 1999 from Adey and Shayer, using value-added data which controls for school intakes, have consistently shown pupils participating in the CASE intervention programme during Key Stage 3 to achieve significantly higher grades at GCSE examinations in science, mathematics and English than matched control groups. Research on subsequent programmes as:

- CAME[4] (cognitive acceleration through mathematics education)
- CATE (cognitive acceleration through technology education)
- PCAME (CAME for top primary – year 5 and 6 in England)
- Let's think!
- LLTS (let's think through science)

[4] Interestingly, a study on the effects on CASE and CAME in Finland also showed significant immediate gains in cognitive development see Hautamäki, J., Kuusela, J. and Wikström, J. (2002, July) *CASE and CAME in Finland: 'The second wave.'* Paper presented at the 10th International Conference on Thinking, Harrogate, UK.

- CAME for Years 1 and 2, cognitive acceleration through arts for Key Stage 3

also show positive effects.[5]

Finally, a comment on the debate around whether 'whole-class' or 'group activity' should dominate, or what should be the balance between whole-class, small group, and individual activities (Joyce et al. 1997: 16). Settling that question leads to the broader question of what will work best for children, because it is the models of learning and teaching that are chosen, rather than the grouping arrangements adopted, that will directly affect student achievement. In these classes, students are taught directly models for learning that they use when working as members of the class community, when working in small collaborative groups and when working as individuals. The more efficient models of teaching assume that the whole class will be organized to pursue common learning objectives within which individual differences in achievement are comfortably accommodated. Thus, the teacher will have a vision of the whole class and a vision of small groupwork and individual work as part of the overall educational scheme. Thus, as Bruce Joyce elegantly phrased it, the operational repertoire of the teacher is the critical element in the calculus of effects.

Continuing professional development of teachers

The question then becomes how to make these teaching behaviours so necessary for personalized learning commonplace for all teachers. The learning and teaching engagements just described tend to be evident in schools that have a culture characterized by high expectations, collaboration and innovation.

This is often referred to as the concept of 'school capacity' that can be described as the collective competency of the school to bring about effective

---

[5] See Adey, P., Nagy, F., Robertson, A., Serret, N. and Wadsworth, P. (2003) *Let's Think through Science!* London: NFERNelson.

Adey, P., Robertson, A. and Grady, V. (2002) Effects of a cognitive acceleration programme on Year 1 pupils, *British Journal of Educational Psychology*, 72(1): 1–25. In 2002 children through CASE in year 1 in Primary schools made significant gains in cognitive development in comparison to the controls.

Adey, P., Robertson, A. and Venville, G. (2001) *Let's Think!* Slough: NFERNelson.

Cassell, A. and Kilshaw, D. (2004) *CAME Maths Project Department for Education and Skills.* www.standards.dfes.gov.uk/giftedandtalented/goodpractice/cs/camemaths/. A school's case study showing pupils' improving on a range of areas as thinking skills, attention and confidence.

Chongde, L., Weiping, H., Philip, A. and Jilian, S. (2003) The influence of CASE on scientific creativity, *Research in Science Education*, 33(2): 143–62. The results indicated that the CASE programme did promote the overall development of scientific creativity of secondary school students with long-lasting effects.

change (Newman et al. 2000). It was suggested that this was compromised of four core components:

- *knowledge, skills and dispositions* of individual staff members
- *a professional learning community* in which staff work collaboratively to set clear goals for student learning, assess how well students are doing, develop action plans to increase student achievement, while being engaged in inquiry and problem solving
- *curriculum coherence* – the extent to which the school's curriculum programme for student and staff learning are coordinated, focused on clear learning goals and sustained over a period of time
- *technical resources* – high-quality curriculum and instructional materials, assessment instruments, technology, workspace etc.

This four-part definition of school capacity includes 'human capital', i.e. the skills of *individuals*, but no amount of professional development of individuals will have an impact if certain *organizational* features are not in place. The key organizational feature in this conceptualization is 'professional learning communities'. These are the 'social capital' aspect of capacity. In other words, the skills of individuals can only be realized if the *relationships* within the schools are continually developing.

The evidence from schools with high levels of student achievement and teacher engagement demonstrates how they build infrastructures for staff development within their day-to-day arrangements. This involves devoting portions of the school week to staff development activities such as curriculum development and implementation, discussion of teaching approaches, regular observation sessions and on-site coaching.

In terms of contemporary professional development practice, the range of professional development activities necessary for effective school improvement are:

- workshops run inside the school on teaching strategies by teachers from the school and collaborating schools, together with some external support
- Whole-staff in-service days on teaching and learning and school improvement planning as well as 'curriculum tours' to share the work done in departments or working groups
- inter-departmental meetings to discuss teaching strategies
- opportunities for the 'school improvement group' or similar to take training and to plan
- partnership teaching, modelling and peer coaching
- the design and execution of collaborative enquiry activities, which are, by their nature, knowledge generating.

The research on staff development identifies a number of key training components which, when used in combination, have much greater power than when they are used alone.[6] The major components of training are:

- presentation of theory or description of skill or strategy
- modelling or demonstration of skills or models of teaching
- practice in simulated and classroom settings
- structured and open-ended feedback (provision of information about performance)
- coaching for application (hands-on, in-classroom assistance with the transfer of skills and strategies to the classroom).

It is also helpful to distinguish between the locations in which these various forms of staff development are best located – either in the 'workshop' or the 'workplace'. The workshop, which is equivalent to the best practice on the traditional professional development course, is where teachers gain *understanding*, see *demonstrations* of the teaching strategy they may wish to acquire and have the opportunity to *practise* them in a non-threatening environment. If the aim is to transfer those skills back into the workplace – the classroom and school – then merely attending the workshop is insufficient. The research evidence is very clear: that skill acquisition and the ability to transfer vertically to a range of situations require 'on-the-job-support'. This implies changes to the workplace and the way in which staff development is organized. In particular, this means the opportunity for *immediate and sustained practice, collaboration and peer coaching* and *studying development and implementation*.

The paradox is that changes to the workplace cannot be achieved without, in most cases, drastic alterations in the ways in which schools are organized. Yet, the transfer of teaching skills from professional development sessions to classrooms settings will not occur without them.

This is a wide range of staff development activity and represents a fairly sophisticated infrastructure for sustained professional development. An important element in all of this is the provision of in classroom support or 'peer coaching'. It is the facilitation of peer coaching that enables teachers to extend their repertoire of teaching skills and to transfer them from different classroom settings to others. The important point is that unless the coaching arrangement involves modelling it appears to have little impact on teachers' behaviour. In our experience, peer coaching is helpful when:

- curriculum, teaching and assessment are the content of staff development

---

[6] This discussion is based on the insights in Joyce, B.R. and Showers, B. (1995) *Student Achievement through Staff Development*, 2nd edn. New York: Longman; and Joyce, B.R., Calhoun, E.F. and Hopkins, D. (1999) *The New Structure of School Improvement*. Buckingham: Open University Press.

- workshops are designed to develop understanding and skill
- school-based groups use modelling of specific models to help attain 'transfer of training'
- peer coaching teams are relatively small, say, two to four members
- the entire staff as well as heads and deputies participate in training and practice
- formative study of student learning is embedded in the process.

There is now an increasingly rich literature on coaching as a means to professional development and its positive effects on teaching and learning. An international systematic review of literature on the impact of collaborative CPD[7] on teaching and learning found teachers having greater confidence, higher involvement in accessing research, self-efficacy and commitment in changing their practice among others. Students were found to have greater motivation, increased sophistication in their answers, more positive response to specific subjects, better organization in their work and better attainment and performance (Cordingley et al. 2003).

In summary, the design of staff development that leads to enhanced levels of student achievement needs to be based on the following principles. It is these features that are in place in schools that are on the road to greatness and that seem most able to personalize learning:

- Make space and time for enhancing teacher enquiry and creating a 'professional practice'.
- Utilize evidence of research and practice in developing a range of teaching models that impact on student learning.
- Study their impact on student learning and use data formatively and habitually.
- Invest in school-based processes (e.g. SIG, triads, modelling /coaching) for extending teacher repertoire.
- Link the classroom focus with whole-school development and imbed pedagogic innovation within curriculum plans.
- Use this emerging 'professional practice' as a basis for networking and system-wide capacity building.

Coda: moving teacher professional development to scale

For every school to become a great school and the teacher skills supportive of personalized learning to become commonplace requires cultural change not

[7] Collaborative CPD was defined as teachers working with at least one other related professional on more than a one-off basis.

just in individual schools but system wide. At a systems level that means both driving demand for high-quality, effective CPD and connecting this to an appropriate supply. By linking demand and supply at the system level the possibility of culture change becomes more real.

The demand side needs to encompass both teacher-level demand and school-level demand and processes are needed for both.

At the teacher level, the key source of demand should spring from some form of regular teaching and learning review. These should be focused on day in day out classroom practice, subject knowledge, effective subject-specific pedagogy and supported by analysis of rich data on pupil performance. The logic here is that the review leads inexorably on to relevant CPD for the teacher, thus locking CPD as well as the review into a single conversation. Teachers will see reviews as a right, because they are keen for feedback, and see CPD as a duty, because they want to improve. They will seek out 'advanced skill' and other experienced teachers for help for the same reason. Every school should expect their best teachers to coach, model and mentor others and demonstrate how they have developed their expertise. All this can be reflected in pay and career progression frameworks.

So, this leads to a simple, but critical question underpinning the new teacher professionalism: has the teacher got the right skills, abilities, knowledge and understanding? Does that include the right subject knowledge, and expertise in terms of generic and subject specific pedagogy?

If the answer is yes, the subsequent question is: what is happening to ensure they fulfil a responsibility to coach, model and mentor others, i.e. become part of CPD supply?

If the answer is no, the question becomes: what CPD is arising from the reviews to help the teacher develop?

At school level, the key source of demand should spring from their own self-evaluation and the system-wide arrangements for inspection and support. In England, for example, this would occur as part of the new relationship with schools: in particular, the new inspection arrangements based on self-evaluation, the publication of the school profile and the single conversation and the pressure brought to bear by the work of the school improvement partner (SIP). This process is facilitated by school-level data that show whether particular subject departments or curriculum areas are falling behind: (a) national standards of achievement by other such departments or areas; (b) standards for benchmarked comparators (e.g. other schools with similarly disadvantaged pupils); (c) other departments or areas in the same school working with the same pupils.

Another potentially powerful demand-side strategy for both primary and secondary schools is the opportunity to take on system-wide roles and be recognized as such. We will discuss these in more detail in Chapter 7, but they could include partnering a failing school, playing a leading role in innovation in their subject in their local area, bringing together groups of locally interested parties to provide extended services in a community and so on. Assuming that these roles are nationally recognized, requirements could be built into the status to make sure that the school is developing as a professional learning community – that their internal professional development work is healthy, robust and effective.

The purpose of these demand-side influences is to create a school-based CPD culture which uses the best teachers to develop others. Such a culture is based on the appreciation that effective professional development involves a balance between gaining access to innovative practice and then applying it in classroom settings. The coaching, modelling and mentoring – essential for sustained change in classroom practice – will necessarily involve interactions during the school day. As we have seen, these patterns of professional practice are still not commonplace in all our schools, but could be incentivized through these demand-side strategies.

At the heart of any supply-side model where schools lead reform will be a mixed market of providers. With more funding and power in the hands of schools, and the muscular demand-side measures just described, the major engine for supply will be demand itself. Schools on the path to greatness and their teachers will have an increasingly clear picture of what they want and need in terms of effective CPD. They will also be clear that CPD will be an activity focused on the classroom and that in-school support will be most important.

There will always be a place for some external support and training; but in a mixed market there will inevitably be some *gaps and discontinuities* in supply. Consequently, the supply-side provision will be differentiated if not at times somewhat messy. It will however need to include the work of 'advanced skill teachers' or similar role, the external support and established CPD provision provided by national agencies and their link with local authorities, the contribution of the subject specialist organizations, the networks of closer support facilitated by national organizations, the role of higher education institutions; and local and other providers.

This proposal can be summarized in Table 4.3.

It is the deliberate use of a range of teaching and learning strategies rich in metacognitive content that will most effectively raise standards of learning and achievement. These teaching and learning strategies are however not 'free floating'; they need to be embedded in the schemes of work and curriculum content that teachers use to structure their lessons. They also have the potential to be shared between schools and be available for wider dissemination. This, of course, is the link with the staff development arrangements the school has established that support the emphasis on high expectations, the careful attention to consistency of teaching and the discussion of pedagogy that pervades the culture of effective schools.

Table 4.3   Taking continuing professional development to scale

DEMAND: driver of change	SUPPLY: ensuring provision
On teachers • Teaching and learning reviews • Advanced/senior teacher status • Progression through promotion and pay scales **On schools** • School self-evaluation • Inspections and external accountability • Conversation with 'school improvement partner', inspector or 'significant other' • Opportunity to become an accredited leading school or professional learning community	• Advanced skill teachers or equivalent • National agencies and local authorities • Subject specialist groups • Networks • Higher education institutions • Locally coordinated provision and other providers

The links between effective teaching and the constellation of staff development activities just described make the structural link between the classroom behaviour of teachers, professional development and enhanced levels of student achievement clear and achievable. In the following chapter, we discuss 'intelligent accountability' and the formative use of data, because these provide the capacity for diagnosis on which the approach to teacher professionalism described in this chapter is predicated.

5 Intelligent accountability

The recent history of educational reform is unequivocal as to the need for a degree of national prescription in its early stages. The argument of the book is that this needs to be balanced with schools leading and taking responsibility for systemic improvement. The nature of the balance will vary according to context. This is particularly the case in relation to accountability. In the move from 'prescription' to 'professionalism' any accountability framework needs to be able not only to fulfil its original purpose, but also to build capacity and confidence. This is not just in terms of its own remit but also in supporting the capacity building function of the other three drivers. How the concept of 'accountability' evolves through the phases of system development and in the process becomes increasingly intelligent is the key issue addressed in this chapter.

A fairly sophisticated national framework for accountability has evolved in England since the early 1990s. That framework, which links together standardized achievement tests and examinations, target setting, publication of performance tables and independent inspection has no doubt made a major contribution to the raising of standards during the period. Michael Barber (2004: 4–5), part-architect and staunch advocate of our system of external accountability, claims that:

> *For pupils and the performance of the system the benefits have been huge. Standards of achievement have been put in the spotlight, expectations have been raised, teachers' efforts have been directed to making a difference and performance has undoubtedly improved.*

Many others, however, have been highly critical of the accountability framework. Although many of these critiques have been the predictable opposition of the unreconstructed and those with vested interests, it is true that such an externally imposed approach to accountability has had some perverse effects. Oft-quoted examples are of teachers 'teaching to the test' and schools increasing their 'competitiveness' through adjusting their admissions policy to boost their position in the published performance tables. Many would also agree that an overemphasis on external accountability increases the degree of dependence and lack of innovation within the system.

But the solution is not to abandon the accountability framework; that would be to throw the baby out with the bath water, but to make it more 'intelligent'. The phrase 'intelligent accountability' was first coined by John Dunford of the Secondary Heads Association (SHA; now the Association of Schools and College Leaders 2003: paragraph 45). SHA defines intelligent accountability as follows:

> Intelligent accountability is a framework to ensure that schools work effect-ively and efficiently towards both the common good and the fullest devel-opment of their pupils. It uses a rich set of data that gives full expression to the strengths and weaknesses of the school in fulfilling the potential of pupils. It combines internal school processes with levels of external monitoring appropriate to the state of development of each individual school.

To better support progress towards 'every school a great school' and to provide the diagnostics to support personalized learning, a more intelligent accountability framework needs to achieve a more even balance between external and internal accountability. Most forms of accountability are exter-nally dominated – the clarification of expected standards at various ages, the setting of targets to be met, the publication of results at school and local level and the use of inspection schemes to ensure quality. Once in place these pillars of the external accountability framework are often difficult to dismantle.

Because of the resilience of external forms of accountability, it is often necessary to compensate by increasing the emphasis on internal forms of accountability. The most common approaches would be the use of teacher assessment, bottom-up target setting, value-added measures of school per-formance and the school holding itself publicly accountable through publish-ing its own profile of strengths and weaknesses and benchmark comparisons giving a more rounded picture of the school's performance. It is these forms of accountability that (a) allow a sharper fix on the focus of personalization and (b) develop the professional skill of the teaching staff involved. As a consequence, when the balance between external and internal account-ability become more even, it also becomes more 'intelligent.' The assumption also is that, over time, as schools increasingly lead reform, internal forms of accountability will become the more important.

Before exploring this territory in a little more detail, it is necessary to do some ground clearing. The debates about accountability are so heated, both within and between countries, that the real issues often become clouded. The argument tends to become ideological and theological rather than a strategic assessment of what is needed in a system to ensure movement towards personalisation and every school becoming great.

So, in this chapter, before exploring the components of an intelligent accountability system, I will:

- first, examine the arguments for and against accountability and short-term targets and
- second, define some of the key terms in the debate.

After looking at the above, I can then describe some of the basic elements of a system of intelligent accountability, in particular:

- how to best balance internal and external forms of assessment and accountability
- approaches to assessment for learning
- forms of self-evaluation underpinning a new relationship with national authorities
- a brief coda on the role of students.

For and against accountability and the tyranny of targets

In attempting to give a sense of the range of the debate for and against accountability, let me quote again from the paper by Michael Barber (2004: 5–6) that was referred to earlier. There he talked about the benefits to students, here he talks about the benefits to teachers:

> *Overall, certainly in England, I am in no doubt that the development of a powerful accountability system has been hugely beneficial for teachers. It has clarified their mission for a start, rather than leaving them thinking they could be all things to all people, the solution to every social and economic problem the country faces. It has made publicly clear over and over again that teachers make a difference, a point often forgotten in the preceding era. It is sometimes assumed that when there is, for example, a heavy intervention in a failing school, the message to the public about teachers is a negative one. In fact, the opposite is the case: such an intervention is a clear statement of the value of good teachers and good schools. It is the neglect of failure that undermines the public's perception of teachers.*
>
> *There is another point too. The data generated by accountability is the key to enhancing professional knowledge about best practice. Accountability has therefore moved the whole concept of professionalism forward. Instead of a myriad of bottom-up boutique projects, which may or may not work and the lessons of which may or may not be disseminated, we now have the*

capacity through benchmarking not just for each school to identify its strengths and weaknesses but for the system to identify best practices and to invest in their systematic dissemination. This creates the foundation of a new, informed professionalism.

The final and most important benefit of accountability for teachers is that it has created the possibility of a virtuous circle, connecting teachers to the public. It establishes goals which the public can understand and believe in; it provides feedback to the public so they can see the benefits of their investment; and because it causes the system to address its weaknesses, it creates continuous improvement which encourages the public to keep faith.

All of this sounds eminently reasonable, even to one who as a young teacher in the 1970s had firsthand experience of an 'accountability-free' system. As a teacher educator in the 1980s and 1990s I was close to teachers' (mainly negative) reactions to the introduction of a national accountability framework. But in my naivety, I had assumed that much of the antagonism towards accountability had dissipated during the recent past and was now regarded as a helpful way of personalizing learning and enhancing professionalism. I was therefore a little surprised when in government during New Labour's second term to realize the degree of antipathy with which many teacher unions and academics regard the various approaches to accountability. Space and sensitivity precludes a full analysis, but it is important to get a flavour of the debate.

Take for example this extract from a report on accountability by the Association of Teachers and Lecturers (ATL) – one of England's more moderate teacher unions:

> *The nature and pace of change, particularly since the election of a Labour government in 1997, has unnecessarily increased teacher workload, which they have found unhelpful in supporting children's learning. It has also prompted many teachers to leave their jobs. . . . If the pressures of testing and league tables are maintained, together with the pressures of other external accountability audit mechanisms, then these are likely to continue to have a negative impact on the processes of teaching and learning, and the well-being of teachers and their pupils. . . . ATL believes that we need to reclaim the professional ground that we have lost. We must also be clearer about accountability mechanisms, ensuring that teachers are accountable to those who really matter – the children and their parents, society and the profession – and for the things that really matter: children's learning, development and well-being.*

(Webb and Vulliamy 2006: 14, 16)

Before reflecting on this quote let us also look at the views of academics. Andy Hargreaves is currently one of the best known and articulate writers and speakers on educational matters. Born in Lancashire and having taught as a primary school teacher, he now has a worldwide reputation as an educator. In a recent book, written with Dean Fink, *Sustainable Leadership* (2006: 253–54), he forcibly argues that 'short term achievement targets transgress every principle of sustainable leadership and learning'. The authors support their argument in this way:

1 *Depth. Short-term targets push most schools to focus on testing before learning; they put a priority only on learning that is easily measured; they narrow learning to the old basics, sacrificing breadth as well as depth, and by turning a sense of urgency into a state of fear and panic, they short-circuit teacher learning and replace it with paint-by-numbers training.*

2 *Length. Government ministers and the system leaders who implement their mandates frequently find they are unable to deliver the targets on time – and then their jobs are gone. Some do reach the targets by forcing or faking them, but the results quickly plateau once the system has run out of tricks. Leaders are cycled in and out of schools with increasing frequency in the hope that a few will emerge who can produce miracle solutions, but accelerating succession only plunges schools into doom loops of performance decline.*

3 *Breadth. Acceleration and standardization of imposed change and its targets reduces teachers' time for working together and for learning from one another slowly and sustainably, as real learning communities. Distributed leadership turns into downloaded delegation along with artificial additives of stilted learning teams.*

4 *Justice. Target-driven forms of competitive accountability create disincentives for neighbouring schools to share their learning and expertise. The desperate search for heroic stories of exemplary success also encourages systems to exalt highly improving schools at the expense of their neighbours, awarding them preferential allocations of interest, resources, and support.*

5 *Diversity. Imposed, short-term targets turn the deserved focus on deep standards into a damaging fixation with standardized testing. Standardization destroys and denies the diversity among students and teachers that is the source of their strength.*

6 *Resourcefulness. Improvement needs energy – energy that can be conserved and renewed, not used up and drained dry. High-speed implementation driven by short-term targets uses excessive energy, leaves no time for renewal, and causes people to run out of gas.*

7 *Conservation. Short-term targets force us to think and work in the present and future tense. Their creative destruction makes it hard for us to take the time to acknowledge, learn from, and recombine elements from the past, then move beyond them. Imposed, short-term targets turn us into innocent orphans who have been left no legacy and are cast into a world of repetitive and relentless change.*

These two extracts are pretty powerful stuff – as convincing on first reading as is Barber's. Are these positions reconcilable? Where does truth lie? Unfortunately, it is probably the case that the positions are not reconcilable and truth as we have seen, at least in educational debates, is somewhat plastic. In the search for a middle way let us look at some other views.

As we have seen, one of the more constructive contributors to the accountability debate in England has been that of the Secondary Heads Association (now the Association of Schools and College Leaders). I have already quoted John Dunford, the General Secretary, and his definition of intelligent accountability. It is worth tracking their position in a little more detail. SHA's first policy document was published in March 2003 and began by accepting:

> [T]hat proper safeguards are required for the spending of public money and the quality of delivery of public services. The public is entitled to reassurance that funds are being spent with propriety and that the service is efficient and effective.

The SHA document then quickly asserted that:

> Current levels of accountability in education go much further than this. . . . School accountability is very much greater than is necessary to ensure the effectiveness of a public service. This over-accountability increases bureaucracy and acts as a disincentive to creativity. SHA believes that the government should review the accountability of schools and examine ways in which a slimmer accountability·regime could better support schools in raising achievement and fulfilling their wider aims

In support of this argument Dunford refers to Onora O'Neill's Reith Lecture in 2002 – A Question of Trust – in which she powerfully maintained that the present culture of accountability in the public sector damages trust rather than supports it. She notes that professional people, including teachers, are no longer trusted and believes that 'this crisis of trust is a crisis of suspicion'. Although the pursuit of accountability provides citizens and consumers with more information, it builds suspicion, low morale and professional cynicism. This is very much the position taken by the ATL and Hargreaves and Fink. Dunford's response, however, is somewhat different and he uses the same analysis to argue as we saw earlier for a form of 'intelligent accountability'.

This response is best seen in a later pamphlet where SHA (2004: 1) claims some credit for the government's adopting 'the notion of intelligent accountability and . . . examining how best the current accountability regime could be slimmed down and made more effective'. Dunford then quotes approvingly the speech by the Minister of State for School Standards, David Miliband, in Belfast on 8 January 2004, where in introducing 'the new relationship with schools' he identified three key components of whole school improvement:

> First, an accountability framework, which puts a premium on ensuring effective and ongoing self-evaluation in every school combined with more focused external inspection, linked closely to the improvement cycle of the school; second, a simplified school improvement process, where every school uses robust self-evaluation to drive improvement, informed by a single annual conversation with the education system on targets, priorities and support; and third, improved data flows, including to parents.

I believe that a common thread is appearing here. It is a realization that accountability is a necessary part of a systemic reform strategy in a modern educational system, but that an overreliance on external forms of accountability can have a distorting effect on the system and that a balance between internal and external forms needs to be found. This is the position described by Michael Fullan in the Ontario case described in Chapter 2. Fullan (2006: 48) also commented on the Hargreaves and Fink position:

> My colleagues, Hargreaves and Fink (2006), are against externally imposed targets arguing that they are not owned and result in superficial actions and mistrust. Their argument seems to be around whether the targets are experienced as externally imposed, as they say, 'people can and sometimes should set targets together as part of a shared commitment'.

In this latter frame, when they are owned, targets are at the heart of personalization. If then 'intelligent accountability' is the form of accountability that can help every school become great, we need to look at what a systemic approach looks like in practice. We begin by defining our terms a little more clearly.

Defining terms

When I was in Chile recently the previous Minister of Education Martin Zilic[1] announced that his priorities were standards, assessment and accountability.

---

[1] On 14 July 2006, Chile's Prime Minister Michelle Bachelet removed Education Minister Martin Zilic and replaced him with the former Planning Minister Yazna Provoste. The move was a result of Zilic's poor management of the students' protests in May–June, whose demands included a new curriculum, free bus fare and the removal of exam fees.

This caused some consternation among the teachers and principals with whom I was working as they envisaged some form of draconian style approach to educational change. I was alarmed by the amount of concern these proposals generated and in line with the previous discussion I explained the terms to them in this way.

Standards

This refers to the expected level of performance of a student at the various stages of their school career. The identification of a standard is important for two reasons. First, it enables the student and his/her teachers to know the level they are performing at and to plan accordingly. Most secondary students in England now know the level they are working at as well as the level they are working towards. As a result they are able to take more control over their own learning. This is personalization. The second aspect of standards is that they are educationally meaningful rather than arbitrary. So, for example, in England the expected standard in English at the end of primary education is Level 4. 'Level four-ness' reflects the level of performance necessary to access the secondary curriculum; without reaching this standard the student would struggle in secondary education. Seen in this light, standards become an important tool for personalized learning and for ensuring equity.

Assessment

This describes the process by which the attainment of a standard is measured. This is commonly of two types – internal and external assessment. The former usually relates to assessment undertaken by a student's school, college or other provider, commonly referred to as teacher assessment; and the latter to a national standardized exam, externally marked. Both can be used in a formative or a summative way.

Formative assessment is commonly understood as assessment for learning and this has a clear focus on the improvement of learning. This is an essential feature of personalization; learning how to learn is an embedded component of effective teaching and lays the basis for school self-evaluation. In terms of formative assessment, there is a need to develop increasingly precise methods for assessment for learning, pupil progress data, contextual value added and school profiles. These can become tools not just for personalizing learning and enhanced teacher professionalism, but also for assisting school self-evaluation and holding schools open to public scrutiny.

Summative assessment, by the same token, is commonly understood as assessment of learning whose uses are certification, selection, standard setting and accountability. In terms of summative assessment, there is a case for considering random national sampling, which can be a more effective means of monitoring the level of national standards than full cohort testing, which is onerous, expensive and has too wide a margin of error.

The operational clarity between formative and summative assessment enables each to more effectively support their core purpose, particularly when techniques most often associated with either internal or external assessment can be used for both formative or summative purposes.

Accountability

This is another of those educational terms that is subject to a high degree of conceptual pluralism. As long ago as 1980 when the winds of accountability began to blow across the educational landscape in England, Hugh Sockett (1976) made some helpful distinctions about the term. He admitted that the simple definition of accountability that of 'holding someone to account' belied significant differences in both practice and meaning. A key tension in the term is whether the purpose of accountability is to improve quality or performance on the one hand (formative) or to prove that some has been done or achieved on the other (summative). Of course, it is both, but the failure to differentiate leads to high levels of confusion in both practice and strategy. The other distinction that Sockett advanced was accountability in terms of results (external) or in terms of professional codes of practice (internal). Taking both these distinctions together with the previous discussion gives us a two-by-two matrix that clarifies some of the confusion in debates over account-ability. A framework for thinking about the two dimensions of formative and summative assessment and internal and external accountability is seen in Figure 5.1.

The real difficulty is that in general people do not specify which type of accountability they are referring to when they use the term or implement an approach. The argument here is that intelligent accountability embraces the range of these definitions rather than just internal or external, formative or summative and is about getting the balance between each of them right. The right balance is not set, it is not a given but, as we see later, depends on context.

Balancing internal and external assessment and accountability

In drawing a picture of an intelligent accountability framework, it is necessary to talk in very concrete terms. As we have seen, the issue is so emotional that unless we talk about practicalities, issues often become clouded. In doing this, I will inevitably draw on my experience in England, where I was partially responsible for helping that system move from one dominated by external forms of accountability to one where there was a better balance between that

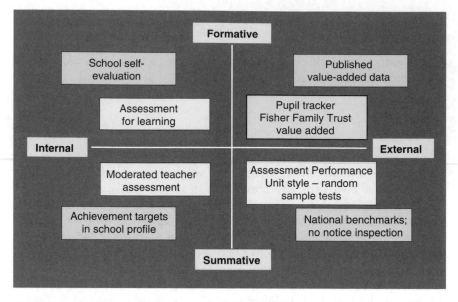

Figure 5.1 Balancing internal and external accountability

and internal forms. It became very clear to me in my early days as a civil servant that dismantling the accountability framework was not an option and that one had to build on and evolve from existing arrangements – hence the need to introduce balance.

Before I go any further let me state clearly that I am not advocating the English framework as an ideal. My own view is that although there were good reasons to start with a fairly robust external framework, we should have introduced the opportunity for more balance earlier than we did. Had we done this, we may have avoided some of the more perverse effects that Hargreaves and Fink so graphically described. The English case, however, does serve to raise issues that are generalizable to other contexts, so I will briefly continue.

As I have said, in the mid-1990s the accountability framework in England was well established on the four pillars of tests, targets, tables and inspection and were dominated by its external forms. A summary of this position is seen in the left-hand column of Table 5.1. For reasons that should by now be clear we moved towards a situation in 2004 where a better balance has achieved as seen in the middle column of Table 5.1.

The direction of travel is as in the right-hand column clear:

- *Tests* – a mixed economy with a presumption of external testing in core subjects at key stages, but with a gradual move to teacher assessment in other cases.

Table 5.1 Summary of the accountability framework in England pre-1997, in 2004 and in the future

	Pre-1997	*2004*	*Future*
Tests	External/summative tests at KS1–3, GCSE and A level	External (with pilots in teacher assessment)/ summative (with drive on AfL)	Synergy between formative and summative: external and internal
Targets	Top-down/school-level, but no targets required at KS1 and 2	Top-down at KS3 and GCSE. Bottom-up at KS1–2/improved pupil-level data	Bottom-up, school owned/ student-level to drive individual performance
Tables	Raw data at KS2, GCSE and A level	Raw and value added from KS2 to GCSE	Raw results and contextual value added
Inspection	External/detailed, long notice, massive preparation	External/focused: shorter notice, significant preparation	External/focused, combined with self-evaluation

- *Target setting* – with a move to bottom-up school-owned targets, informed by individual student-level data, to drive up performance.
- *Tables* – with a move to contextual value-added tables combined with the school profile to give a clear picture of progress.
- *Inspection* – with a move to short duration inspections with minimal observation, informed by self-evaluation; small teams; and a short, sharp report with clearer recommendations for improvement.

Despite this, critics still remain. The ATL together with most teacher unions still have major reservations about the publication of performance tables and the concerns with targets as a lever of reform are enduringly contentious. Such debates are inevitable and are probably a characteristic of any evolving educational system.

One of the issues not fully resolved in the accountability settlement in England, however, is that of testing. As has been seen there is currently a mixed economy with the balance of testing shifting from internal to external as students move through school stages. Looked at from the perspective of the previous two drivers, there are strong arguments for moderated teacher assessment being the default approach to assessment. It can be very reliable and links well to personalized learning, supports teacher professionalism and through external moderation encourages the transfer of curriculum innovation between schools. As the effectiveness and reliability of teacher assessment and school self-evaluation increases, capacity is built in to the system and the need for 'high-stakes' testing can be confined to key points of transition in a narrower range of subjects. This would leave the opportunity open for schools to be responsible for their own assessment through a chartered examiner approach, with a possible return to an Assessment of Performance Unit (APU) model of randomized sampling.

The way in which the accountability system has evolved to better balance internal and external accountability is seen in Table 5.2. It represents a reasonable if not ideal balance between internal and external assessment and provides a platform for building capacity and professional accountability towards the next phase of reform.

One last point. This settlement was not easy to achieve and was inevitably politically contentious. This will always be the case. The problem is that changes to the accountability framework are usually achieved piecemeal rather than as a big bang or part of a strategic and purposeful rebalancing. Because of this opponents of accountability will perceive the framework as continuously open to change through attrition. This is inevitably destabilizing and no way to build a platform for schools leading reform.

Table 5.2 A framework for building intelligent accountability

	Internal	*External*
Tests	Assessment for learning using a range of tools at all ages Teacher assessment at KS1	External tests at KS1, KS2 and KS3 Test results published at KS2–3
Targets	Targets for every child – part of the learning culture Self-evaluation identifies priority areas for targets and action Use pupil performance data to inform target levels	Schools must set targets at KS2–4 High-quality data means LEA can check targets are stretching Floor targets bite on low performers
Tables	VA and CVA help establish strengths/weaknesses relative to peers	Raw at KS2, KS3, GCSE and A Level VA at KS2-GCSE and KS3-GCSE
Inspection (2005/06)	Rigorous self-evaluation throughout school required to demonstrate sound management to OfSTED	Every 3 years at no notice More frequent in weak schools HMI oversee all inspections

It is therefore important to make clear that the move towards 'intelligent accountability' is part of an explicit strategy in pursuit of personalization, building capacity within the system and in ensuring that every school is great. In the following two sections, we look in more detail at 'assessment for learning' and 'school self-evaluation' as the two most prominent strategies for achieving this.

Assessment for learning

For every school to be a great school we need to move from standardized provision with uncontrolled variation in quality to personalized provision based on consistently high quality, where variation is controlled and actively tailored to individual pupils' needs and aspirations. This is to ensure that the achievement of full potential becomes universal. The most powerful lever we can pull at the moment to achieve personalized learning is assessment for learning.

Personalized learning depends on teachers (and students) knowing in a deep way the strengths and weaknesses of individual students. Assessment for learning has been defined by the Assessment Reform Group (2002) as:

> *The process of seeking and interpreting evidence for use by learners and their teachers to decide where the learners are in their learning, where they need to go and how best to get there.*

This may be organized differently in different schools, but the rationale must always be the same:

- clear evidence about how to drive up individual attainment
- clear feedback for and from pupils so there is clarity on what they need to improve and how best they can do so
- clarity for students on what grades/levels they are working at, with transparent criteria to enable peer coaching
- a clear link between student learning and lesson planning.

Since assessment for learning is a key component of personalized learning, a large part of the success of personalized learning and the fulfilment of the radical agenda for change it presents will depend on whether high-quality assessment for learning can be developed powerfully and consistently through the education system. Assessment for learning therefore:

- provides a framework to help structure and focus the whole school development of teaching and learning

- gives teachers a shared language and context within which they can develop their teaching skills, such as questioning, modelling, explaining and providing informative oral and written feedback
- helps establish a learning environment in which the respective roles and responsibilities of pupils and teachers are better understood, and pupils increasingly take responsibility for their progress and becoming more actively engaged.

Central to assessment for learning is the focus on helping pupils become increasingly effective independent learners. Teachers need to develop a good understanding of subject progression so that they can help pupils:

- understand precisely what they are trying to learn and why, and what their next steps are
- assess their own progress (and similarly help their peers)
- recognize the standards they are aiming for and strive for personal excellence.

Teachers also need to continue to develop their understanding of how pupils learn so that they can help them to:

- reflect on how they learn
- develop learning strategies and apply them in different circumstances
- engage in high-quality classroom dialogue with the teacher, other adults and their peers in order to develop as effective independent learners.

There are few schools where we could say that assessment for learning is presently well established across all classes and teachers to reach all pupils. Nevertheless, although significant gains have been made and there are examples of outstanding practice. For example, OFSTED (2004) identifies assessment and its application to teaching and learning as comparatively weak areas in English schools. Too many schools lack adequate systems for tracking the progress of individual pupils.

We need to develop the strategies and techniques, but more than this we need to construct a shared understanding nationally and internationally of what assessment for learning entails and of how it sits within teaching and learning. We need to be secure in the rationale of how and why it works. In this regard we have been well served of late. The OECD project on Formative Assessment (CERI 2005: 43–51) provided us with such data – through case studies research and an examination of international literature – in eight education systems. The research concluded that formative assessment is one of the most useful strategies in improving student performance and identified the following practices as ones that consistently emerged during the project:

- establishment of classroom cultures that encourage interaction and the use of assessment tools
- establishment of learning goals and tracking individual student progress toward goals
- use of varied instruction methods to meet diverse student needs
- use of varied approaches to assess student understanding
- feedback on student performance and adaptation of instruction to meet identified needs
- active involvement of students in the learning process.

In England, there have been exciting developments in recent years particularly the work of academics and practitioners based at King's College, London, led by Paul Black and Dylan Wiliam, and the members of the Assessment Reform Group with their seminal Black Box series of research findings.[2] The recent work of Mary James (in press) and her colleagues on practices likely to promote learning how to learn is an important contribution. In England, too, the primary and secondary national strategies are the key delivery platforms for the teaching and learning strand. They are undertaking the largest ever initiative (both nationally and internationally) to support the development of assessment for learning in schools.

Although assessment for learning is about raising standards of learning and achievement, it is also more than this. On the one hand, it forms a major part of a movement towards ensuring 'intelligent accountability' pervades our education system. On the other, it offers the opportunity for a radical redefinition of the culture of classroom practice through building ownership of the teaching and learning process among learners and teachers. This is a point that is also made in a recent book by Michael Fullan, Peter Hill and Carmen Creola (2006) ambitiously entitled *Breakthrough*. In this book, Fullan and his colleagues examine the pedagogic implications underpinning much of Fullan's recent work, some of which we have already reviewed. They come to similar conclusions about the curriculum as were reached in Chapter 3 of the current volume. Simply put, they claim that there are numerous examples of good curriculum that provide the necessary degree of specification and well-designed teaching approaches that work effectively in classroom settings when used at the right time with the right students.

[2] See Black, P. and William, D. (1998) *Inside the Black Box: Raising Standards through Classroom Assessment*. London: King's College London; Assessment Reform Group (1999) *Assessment for Learning: Beyond the Black Box*. Cambridge: University of Cambridge, School of Education; and Black, P., Harrison, C., Lee, C., Marshall, B. and Wiliam, D. (2002) *Working inside the Black Box: Assessment for Learning in the Classroom*. London: NFERNelson. Available from www.assessment-reform-group.org.uk/publications.html (accessed 22 May 2006).

What is missing they argue is the focus on assessment for learning and they identify the four features of classroom practice that are virtually non-existent at the current time. These are:

1   *A set of formative assessment tools tied to the learning objectives of each lesson that give the teacher access to accurate information on the progress of each student on a daily basis, and that can be administered without undue disruption to normal classroom routines.*

2   *A method to allow the formative assessment data to be captured in a way that is not time-consuming; of analyzing the data automatically, and; a means of converting it into information that is powerful enough to drive instructional decisions not sometime in the future, but tomorrow.*

3   *A means of using the assessment information on each student to design and implement lessons that deliver differentiated instruction that optimize the effectiveness of classroom teaching.*

4   *A built-in means of monitoring and managing learning, of testing what works, and of systematically improving the effectiveness of classroom instruction so that it more precisely responds to the learning needs of each student in the class.*

They conclude:

> *One can think of instances where current practice comes close to achieving one or more of the above, but we are aware of none that integrates all four. If classroom instruction could be organized this would lead to quantum, ongoing improvements in the rate of student learning, but more significantly to a transformational change in thinking about teaching. This is because, for the first time, classroom instruction would be organized so that teaching followed the student.*

The last paragraph is particularly exhilarating and evocative. That possibility, however, will only be realized when two conditions are met. First is the necessity to blend curriculum, pedagogy and assessment for learning in transforming the culture of teaching and learning. Second is the imperative to integrate the levels of classroom, school and system in the movement towards personalization and every school becoming a great school. This is the argument underpinning the three-level model introduced in Chapter 1. So, it is appropriate that we turn now to a discussion of the implications of 'intelligent accountability' at the school level.

Self-evaluation and 'new relationships' with schools

Before discussing contemporary approaches to school self-evaluation a short history lesson may be instructive. There was a marked change in the character of school improvement efforts in the late 1970s and early 1980s which was largely the result of an increase in demands for school accountability. In the United Kingdom, for example, the reaction to the pressure for accountability took the form of a variety of local education authority (LEA) schemes for school self-evaluation. At this time it was viewed as one of the few improvement strategies that could not only strengthen the capacity of the school to develop or renew itself, but also provide evidence for accountability purposes and a structure for managing the change process. The OECD International School Improvement Project (ISIP), in particular, took a leading role in conceptualizing and disseminating examples of school evaluation (Bollen and Hopkins 1987; Hopkins 1987, 1988).

Our own research on school self-evaluation efforts at the time suggested that schools find carrying out a full review very time consuming (Hopkins 1987). We also found that there was an apparent lack of rigour and objectivity and more importantly school self-evaluation had difficulty in impacting directly on classroom practice. It was for these reasons that we began to advocate more comprehensive strategies for self-evaluation – development planning.

In England in 1989 when the then DES issued its first advice, development planning was regarded as a means of helping schools manage the extensive national and centrally driven change agenda and also enabling schools 'to organise what it is already doing and what it needs to do in a more purposeful and coherent way'. Priorities for development are planned in detail for one year and are supported by action plans that are the working documents for teachers. The priorities for subsequent years are sketched in outline to provide the longer term programme. An overview of the planning process is seen in Figure 5.2 (Hargreaves et al. 1989: 4).

Research[3] into school improvement during the 1990s showed that schools that exhibited best practice in development planning used it as a strategy to enhance directly the progress and achievement of students. The focus was on students' learning, their progress and achievement; what was needed to improve it and how this was best supported. Crucial to this shift was the closer integration of implementation and evaluation as illustrated in Figure 5.2 and the use of the teachers' professional judgement.

In *The Empowered School*[4] (1991) David Hargreaves and I argued that the

[3] See MacGilchrist et al. (1995); Hopkins et al. (1996); MacGilchrist et al. (1997).

[4] See Chapter 9 in Hargreaves, D. and Hopkins, D (1991) *The Empowered School: The Management and Practice of Development Planning*. London: Cassell.

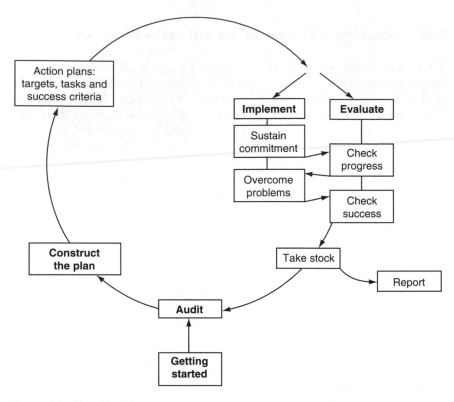

Figure 5.2   The planning process

process of checking on progress and success in development planning requires teachers to use their professional judgement in a systematic way. It is not the mechanistic completion of progress and success checks that is important, but rather it is the enhancing of the teachers' professional judgement that is the crucial aspect of embedding an ethos of enquiry and reflection within a school. This process provides the interface between assessment for learning, self-evaluation, development planning and school improvement.

Teachers already monitor and evaluate their own actions as well as the behaviour and work of pupils as part of their everyday activities. If teachers did not rely on their *intuitive professional judgement*, they would not be able to cope with the complexities of their work. There are occasions, however, when it cannot be wholly relied on as a basis for making a decision. In these circumstances, teachers make a *considered professional judgement*, which requires some action to check the intuitive judgement. A considered professional judgement is reached through reflection and further investigation. Both are a natural and inherent part not only of assessing progress for evaluation but more generally as a key feature of the school improvement process.

The move towards personalized learning however will often create new working circumstances with which the teacher is less familiar. In these cases a *refined professional judgement* is required. This is an opportunity for enhancing professional judgement and is achieved:

- through discussion with colleagues about the extent of progress or success in school improvement work
- by establishing agreement on standards used to make judgements
- through mutual observation in the classroom
- through the use of informed opinion.

Extending teachers' professional judgements therefore links the professional development of the individual teacher to the development of the school as a whole as well as improving the quality of teaching and learning. It is in this way that the three drivers of personalization, professionalism and intelligent accountability become mutually supportive.

So although school self-evaluation lost popularity during the late 1980s and early 1990s, it is now enjoying a renaissance. This seems to be due to its links to student learning where the work of John Macbeath (1999) is important, the enhancing of teachers' professional judgement, whole-school improvement and, as we shall see, new forms of inspection.

The contribution of this enhanced, more holistic and contemporary approach to school self-evaluation to intelligent accountability in England is most concretely expressed in the 'new relationship with schools.' As we have already noted this was announced by David Miliband in his North of England speech in January 2004. He said that personalized learning:

> [W]ill require a new relationship with schools which will give schools the time, support and information they need to focus on what really matters. By strengthening our school improvement process, improving our data flows and working with schools to tackle problems we will ensure there is a real focus on the central priorities of teaching and learning.

There are four key aspects of the new relationship with local educational authorities and schools. These are:

1 *an intelligent accountability* framework which puts a premium on assessment for learning, bottom-up target setting, and ensuring effective and ongoing self-evaluation in every school, combined with a sharper edged, lighter touch external inspection and an annual school profile to complement performance table data
2 *a simplified school improvement process* in which every school uses robust self-evaluation to drive improvement and produces a single

school improvement plan based on a smaller number of DfES output measures. Every secondary school will have access to a dedicated school improvement partner with whom they conduct a single conversation on targets, priorities and support, within the context of three-year budgeting

3 *improved data and information systems* that give schools the chance to take control of the flow of information through an online ordering system for all departmental documents and align the activity of the DfES and its partners to ensure that data are 'collected once, used many times';

4 *a school profile* containing data about student performance and the school's own view of its priorities and performance. It will be light on bureaucracy, easy to access and powerful in impact, supplementing performance tables and replacing the annual statutory report to parents.

This more aligned school improvement process is captured in Figure 5.3.

Central to the 'New Relationship with Schools' (DfES 2004e) in England is the role of schools self-evaluating themselves through the self-evaluation form (SEF). The SEF requires schools to provide evidence on their performance, on their strengths and weakness, to identify precise issues as their key priorities

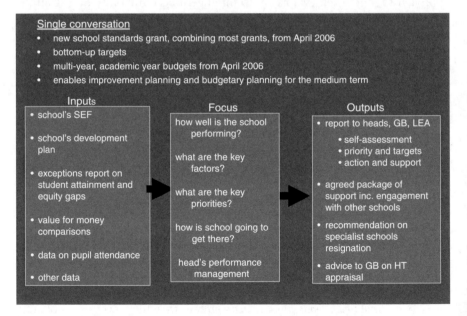

Figure 5.3 The New Relationship with Schools school improvement process

for improvement and to plan how they intend to improve them. These feed into the school improvement plan where schools set specific targets for each of these priorities.

The 'New Relationship with Schools: Improving Performance through Self-evaluation', poses the following questions in the centre of the self-evaluation process. A case study research by OFSTED in 2006 reflected these questions as ones schools used and evaluation was perceived effective (DfES 2004d: 7–10):

- Does the self-evaluation identify how well our school serves its learners?
- How does our school compare with the best schools and the best comparable schools?
- Is the self-evaluation integral to our key management systems?
- Is our school's self-evaluation based on a good range of telling evidence?
- Does our self-evaluation and planning involve key people in the school and seek the views of parents, learners and external advisers and agencies?
- Does our self-evaluation lead to action to achieve the school's longer term goals for development?

Of course, these questions are very important in self-evaluation, but in order to increase the quality of the process we have to be aware that it is a dynamic and continuous one (Blanchard 2002; OFSTED 2006). It constantly needs revisiting, examining and reflecting and evaluating and target setting. This way it becomes more powerful and a part of the school's improvement culture. But we must also realize that schools improvement culture is centred on the experience of its students.

Coda: self-evaluation and the role of students

It needs emphasizing that self-evaluation and school improvement should be informed by pupils. The SEF asks for evidence on pupils' views on the school and how the school responds to them, but more in order to ensure that a good service is provided to its stakeholders. I think that we have not fully grasped the power of pupils' experiences as a means of self-evaluation and school improvement. The international initiative Learning School highlights its importance. Here, international groups of students live and learn together for a year in a school and research aspects of learning in the schools they visit somewhere in the world. The results inform school improvement and evaluation, as well as the students gain an understanding of their own learning processes. The programme gave great insights on teaching and learning practices around the world, provided new perspectives and helped in the schools' improvement. One of the important points here is that not only is students' contribution to the school evaluation process very important, but also that evaluations from a different cultural perspective can be fruitful for schools to prepare themselves – and so their pupils – for the global world (Macbeath et al. 2003). Last but not least, this is another way for schools to be accountable 'intelligently'.

In this chapter, we have looked at the arguments for and against accountability and short-term targets, then defined some of the key terms before describing the main elements of a system of intelligent accountability – focusing on balancing internal and external forms of assessment and accountability; approaches to assessment for learning; and of self-evaluation underpinning a new relationship with national authorities. After establishing the importance of intelligent accountability, we can now move to the next key driver in the transition for every school to become a great school – networking and innovation.

6   Networking and innovation

There is a logic to the sequencing of the chapters in this book. If the goal is 'every school a great school' then only a systemic response will suffice, with personalized learning at its core. We will not achieve personalized learning, however, without a radical shift in our approach to teaching through the expansion of teacher repertoire and the use of evidence. This in itself needs 'intelligent' forms of assessment and accountability to provide data for diagnosis and impetus for change. This all has to take place in and around that organization we call school and these schools need to provide receptive environments for personalized learning. The internal features of the school, its external relationships and its approach to innovation are all necessary features of this receptive environment and provide the focus of this chapter. In the concluding chapters of the book, we will examine the system and the role of leadership.

Over the past 10 years there has been a sea change in the attitude of schools towards networking and collaboration. The competitive ethic between schools engendered in many countries by policies with a strong accountability element which promoted differential funding and freedoms, is gradually being replaced or supplemented by the development of a range of funded and unfunded networks. In the quest for every school becoming a great school this is a necessary trend. This is because networks support improvement and innovation by enabling schools to collaborate on building curriculum diversity, extended services and professional support as well as to develop a vision of education that is shared and owned well beyond individual school gates. In networking lies the basis for system transformation.

The prevalence of networking practice supports the contention that there is no contradiction between strong, independent schools and strong networks, rather the reverse. Effective networks require strong leadership by participating heads or principals and clear objectives that add significant value to individual schools' own efforts. Without this, networks wither and die, since the transaction costs outweigh the benefits they deliver. Neither is there a contradiction between collaboration and competition – many sectors of the economy are demonstrating that the combination of competition and collaboration delivers the most rapid improvements.

But, before we get carried away with our enthusiasm for networking, we need to entertain three very important caveats. The first is that networking is not an end in itself, but a means to an end; that end being enriched learning environments for our children. Too many networks focus on process rather than substance and as a result become little more than talking shops. The second concern is that unless schools are effective at internal networking, at learning from each other and reducing within school variation, then it is unlikely that they will have the capacity to network effectively with each other. This is why we focus on both internal and external networking in this chapter. The third point is that networking, as we see it currently practised in England and other countries, is designed to support rather than challenge the current orthodoxy. Unfortunately, they are most usually agents of conservatism not of transformation. The thesis of this book is that networks need to provide the means of re-imagining the landscape of education.

But this is getting us into quite complex terrain that requires us to begin to question some of our basic assumptions of how schools work, how they work together and how good ideas travel rapidly around the system. In *Educational Epidemic*, David Hargreaves (2003a: 24) similarly questions the utility of the input-process-output model of the effective schools and asks:

> [W]hether this basic organisational framework is still the only, or the best, one within which to pursue the goals of universal secondary education.

He continues:

> I want to use concepts that explain why schools are successful not merely describe the nature of that success (such as having a culture of achievement, or being well led, and so on). If the same concepts can also be used to explain what makes other kinds of organisations or whole social systems such as cities or societies effective and successful, then the relationship between schools and their wider environment is more explicit. Elsewhere I have set out a conceptual framework to help us understand the capacity of schools to produce excellent educational outcomes as a result of the interaction between different forms of capital. The quality of a school is explained in terms of three concepts – intellectual capital, social capital and organisational capital.

One can summarize Hargreaves' definition of intellectual capital, social capital and organizational capital as follows:

- *Intellectual capital* is not only the knowledge, skill and competencies of the staff of a school, but also that of the students, their families and communities. The capacity of a school to mobilize its intellectual capital is critical, for this is what fosters new ideas and creates the new knowledge that leads to successful innovation in making the school more effective.
- *Social capital* consists in the trust that exists between the members of a school and its stakeholders and structurally in the networks that exist within the school and between the school and its external partners. Schools that are rich in social capital have a strong sense of themselves as a community and invest in themselves as professional learning communities.
- *Organizational capital* refers to the ability of those in leadership positions in the school to effectively mobilize resources, in particular knowledge and skill about how to improve a school by making better use of its intellectual and social capital, especially to enhance teaching and learning.

The terms intellectual, social and organizational capital therefore provide us not only with a way of understanding what capacity within a school is, but also how it can be built. Put simply, as David Hargreaves notes, the task of leadership is to relate these three forms of capital to one another. For example, 'intellectual capital' (the knowledge and skills of individuals) will not have sustained impact unless certain social capital features are in place. This is the argument for establishing trust-based relationships and 'professional learning communities'. In other words, the skills of individuals can only be realized if the relationships within the school are continually developing. Similarly, without the leadership arrangements that optimise organizational capital (distributed in nature, networked, empowering of others, respectful of the contribution of both school and community partners) neither of the other two forms of capital (or capacity) can be realized.

We will develop the leadership implications of this analysis in the next chapter, but the key point being made here, is that the right-hand side of the figure first introduced in Chapter 2 and reproduced again as Figure 6.1, envisages a radically different view of the educational landscape than that existing in the left-hand segment of the figure.

In the left-hand side of the diagram top-down and input–output models of organizations and change will suffice. In the middle box, the rebalancing or top-down and bottom-up leads to a more dialectical approach where the limits of centralized authority are being tested and alternative approaches experimented with. In the right-hand box, however, neither will do and what is required are lateral ways of working based on different organizational forms and radically re-imagined forms of governance and responsibility.

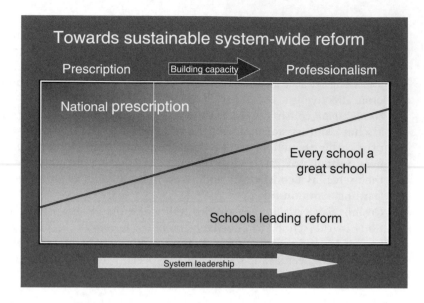

Figure 6.1 Towards sustainable system-wide reform

This is where Hargreaves' concepts have most relevance and purchase. It is also where networking and innovation are vital for progress and enhancing quality.

The problem at the moment is that most forms of organization, networking and innovation are all constrained by 'left-hand box' thinking. They are formulated within an essentially top-down framework. Our task is to re-imagine schools as organizations and networks within the context of right-hand box thinking and ways of working.

This is difficult to do because we are children of our time, but in this chapter an attempt will be made to re-conceive school organization, their ways of working, networking and innovation within a context where it is schools rather than government who lead reform. In doing this, I will:

- make a distinction between a school's maintenance and development functions
- say a word about 'within-school variation'
- describe a model for within-school change
- review some of the evidence on networking
- conclude, in the coda, by reflecting on the nature of innovation and viral ways of working.

Maintenance and development

As schools re-imagine their future as leading reform they will inevitably realize that their existing organizational frameworks are insufficient to sustain the transition. There are two critical issues here:

- The first is: 'Are the "core competencies" for school development in place?' These could be called the school's central nervous system – the features that give confidence that the school can not only achieve its short-term targets and meet the needs of its current students, but can continue to do so over the long term, continuously building its capacity to meet the different challenges it faces.
- The second is the capacity of the school to manage change, evolve and innovate. This requires a school to be able to *maintain* its existing organizational functions to a high degree, but also to have the capacity to *develop* and change. The separation of maintenance activities from development work is essential for the continuous improvement of a school and both need their separate infrastructures. What usually happens, however, is that schools tend to overburden their maintenance system by asking it also to take on development roles for which it was never designed.

Space precludes a detailed discussion of these two issues. This is not, however, to underestimate their importance; the ability of a school to move from one phase of reform to another is essential if we are to create a new educational landscape. In his work on 'strategic leadership', Brent Davies (2005) talks of the ability of the school to improve itself now, but also to build capacity for future development. This is the key capability I am referring to here.

My own summary list of a school's core competencies that is based on both research and practice is found in Table 6.1. Without these features being in place it is unlikely that a school would be effective or able to survive in the short to medium term. These, for example, are the features that inspectors look for in schools to give them confidence that a school can manage the process of teaching and learning, provide good-quality education and can self-evaluate in a robust and realistic way. Although they were originally written with English schools in mind, they also have more general applicability.

But making the transition from one phase of reform to another requires a further capability, that of balancing development and maintenance. In the *Empowered School* (1991: 16), David Hargreaves and I put it this way:

> *Changing a school's culture and approach to management can begin only from where a school now is. At present, schools are facing two kinds of*

Table 6.1   A school's core competencies

Core competencies	Indicators and/or policy areas
Design and delivery of educational programmes tailored to the needs of each student, including the hidden curriculum, social competence and personal confidence	• Personalized learning – tailoring learning and teaching strategies to the needs of each student, ensuring that they are partners in their learning • Primary and secondary strategies – appropriately tailored • Personal and citizenship education – vehicle for developing social competence and personal confidence • Key skills – particularly learning skills as well as other 'soft' skills, which develop 'life' and work competencies
Target setting, assessment, monitoring and reporting on student achievement, which involves the student and includes indicators of student well-being	• Assessment for learning – students involved in the process of identifying targets and learning needs and understand the mechanisms for assessing and reporting on progress against these • Monitoring and reporting of achievement – includes information on students' development as individuals and offers the student opportunity to comment
Resource allocation and facilities management, including all aspects of school design and appearance (especially toilets!)	• Maximizing impact of funding settlement – allocating resources to support school improvement • Schools for the future – capital investment to augment learning outcomes
Performance management and development of all staff, including the establishment of professional learning communities around effective teaching and learning strategies, innovation and the development of problem-solving capacity, within and between schools	• Workforce reform • Pay and performance management – which underpins continuous improvement and ensures that staff feel valued • ITT and CPD – mastery of a range of teaching strategies and awareness of own and students' learning styles • Participation in networks, with time allocated to collaborative learning within and between schools
Stakeholder management, including parental and community relationships	• Collaboration with other local agencies • Engagement of pupils • Involvement of parents – as partners in their children's learning and members of the community, as well as as governors

Strong, but dispersed leadership, based on an explicit statement of values and moral purpose, which are focused on pupil outcomes and clearly communicated throughout the school and to stakeholders

- Dispersed management and leadership – supported through NCSL programmes
- Clear statement of values, ethos and moral purpose in school plan, prospectus etc.
- Effective communication channels

> *pressure. The first is that of development. Schools cannot remain as they now are if they are to implement recent reforms. The second pressure is that of maintenance. Schools need to maintain some continuity with their present and past practices, partly to provide the stability which is the foundation of new developments and partly because the reforms do not by any means change everything the schools now do. There is thus a tension between development and maintenance.*

The ability to balance development and maintenance is provided by what we called in the *Empowered School* the school's 'management arrangements'. They need to support maintenance – the preservation of what has worked well and given the school its stability and reputation. They must also provide a means of dealing with new developments and of creating a new future. We saw three main dimensions to a school's management arrangements:

- *frameworks* that guide the actions of all who are involved in the school
- the clarification of *roles and responsibilities*, so all know what they and others do
- the promotion of ways in which people can *work together*.

These dimensions are highly consistent with the list of core competencies cited earlier. What they fail to do, however, is emphasize sufficiently the need for a developmental infrastructure within the schools as well as those structures that are designed to support maintenance activities. I discussed this issue at length in *School Improvement for Real* and also reproduced the model in Figure 6.2 (Jackson 2000: 64) that illustrates these two separate (yet integrated) structures.

Central to a school's development structure is the 'cadre' or 'school improvement group'. One teacher has described it as the educational equivalent of a research and development group and the traditional school as analogous to a company in which everyone works on the production line, without any research and development function. The result is stagnation and that is how schools have often been. The establishment of a school improvement group creates the research and development capacity, while retaining the existing structures requires both for organizational stability and efficiency. It

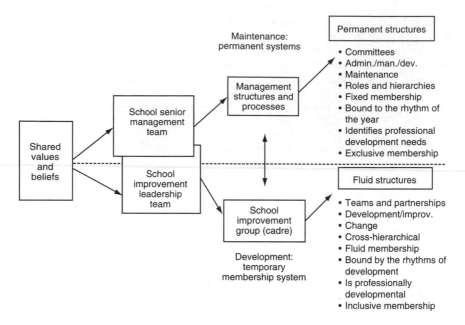

Figure 6.2   Maintenance and development: a model

also unlocks staff potential often stifled within formal structures and opens up opportunities for new forms of collaborations. In organizational terms, a school improvement group is required because of the tensions in schools caused by the conflicting demands of maintenance and development.

Typically, the group is a cross-hierarchical team which could be as small as three or four to six in comparatively small schools, to between six and 10 in large schools. Although one of these is likely to be the head teacher, it is important to establish groups that are genuinely representative of the range of perspectives and ideas available in the school – it should, ideally, then, be cross-hierarchical, cross-institutional, have a mix of ages, experience, gender, length of time at the school and so on. School improvement group members should also not come together in any already existing group within the school, such as the senior management team or a heads of department group, so that the problem of pooled rationalizations is minimized. The cadre group is responsible for identifying the school's improvement focus and for managing efforts on a day-to-day basis within the school. They are supported through a training programme, networking with groups from other schools and by external consultancy support and facilitation.

As we shall see shortly, the school improvement group is the critical structure in establishing an improvement process within the school. Before we turn to this, it is important to address the single most important barrier to the transformation of standards of learning and achievement in schools – the phenomenon of 'within-school variation'.

Within-school variation

Although the current focus on networking and between school collaboration is essential for large-scale systemic change, it may ironically have the perverse effect of deflecting attention from the importance of focusing on within-school variation. Within-school variation refers to the variation in the attainment of pupils in any one school after individual factors, such as socio-economic background, have been accounted for, and reflects the differential impact or effectiveness of individual teachers and curriculum areas. Recent research has highlighted the impact of within-school variation on student achievement, with the PISA study, for example, suggesting that within-school variation in England is some four times greater than the variation between schools (see Figure 6.3). Without a direct focus on within-school variation it is unlikely that we will see a further transformation in standards. The following two diagrams illustrate the issue well. Figure 6.4 demonstrates that it is deprivation that accounts for virtually all the variation between schools rather than the variation within schools. In line with this, Figure 6.5 demonstrates that it is the quality of teaching that accounts for all the significant (and at times sustained) variation of student achievement within schools. Figure 6.6 illustrates the same phenomenon at the school level.

Although it is salutary to find that it is teaching quality that accounts for within-school variation the good news, at least if the argument of this book is to be believed, is that this is something that we can do something about. And if we do, then most schools will be well on their way to being great.

As we saw in Chapter 4, there are two determinants of teaching quality: the nature of effective teaching and the design of staff development. There is no need to reiterate those arguments again here. However, in order to make

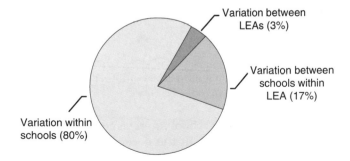

Figure 6.3 At what level in the system does the variation lie?

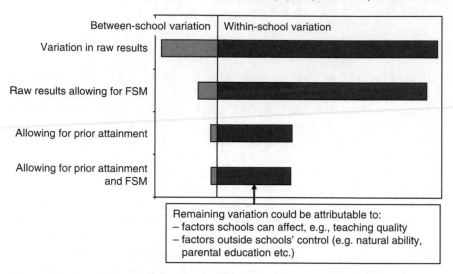

Figure 6.4 Contributors to variation within and between schools

Teaching can affect variance. At KS3 there are disparities at subject level.
Some schools appear to do consistently better in English than maths and vice versa –
evidence of teacher or department level weaknesses

		Better in mathematics than English	2003 Results broadly similar	Better in English than mathematics	
2002	Better in mathematics than English	10%	11%	5%	Consistent difference
	Results broadly similar	11%	30%	11%	
	Better in English than mathematics	4%	9%	8%	

Figure 6.5 Teaching and variation of student achievement within schools at Key Stage 3

the links between (a) the role of a school improvement group as the key development structure in a school and (b) the necessity to reduce within-school variation, it is necessary to establish a school-level improvement process that contains the following range of professional development activities. The

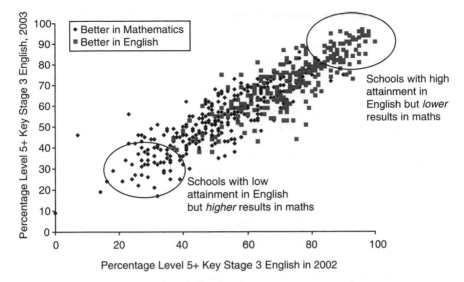

Figure 6.6 Scope for improvement among both high- and low-performing schools

following are the necessary organizational features required for reducing within-school variance:

- regular provision and use of data on student and teacher performance
- workshops on teaching and learning strategies, including demonstration and modelling, to give a precision to the language of teaching used in the school
- inter-departmental meetings to discuss data on student learning and achievement and teaching strategies
- whole-staff in-service days on teaching and learning and school improvement planning as well as 'curriculum tours' to share the work done in departments or working groups
- opportunities for the 'school improvement group' or similar to take training and to plan
- partnership teaching, modelling and peer coaching but organized in triads
- design and execution of cyclical collaborative enquiry activities and data use, which are, by their nature, knowledge generating.

The argument being made here is that if we are to reduce within-school variation such forms of staff development are essential. The links between effective teaching and the constellation of staff development activities just described make the structural link between the classroom behaviour of teachers and enhanced levels of student achievement clear and achievable. An excellent example of work in this area is provided by the National College of School Leaders' Leadership Network. This practical work was supported by research conducted by, among others, David Reynolds (Hopkins et al. 2005).

As I said earlier, it is becoming clear that schools that have learned to collaborate internally are subsequently much more effective at collaborating with other schools. Put another way, without developing strategies for addressing within-school variation schools and teachers will only be able to collaborate at a superficial level. All this sustains the argument being made in this book, that approaches to school improvement need to focus both on the organizational conditions of the school as well as the organization of teaching and learning. The more the organization of the school remains the same the less likely will there be changes in classroom practice that directly and positively impact on student learning. We look in the following section at a strategy designed for addressing just this.

The three phases of school improvement

This approach to school improvement stands in stark contrast to the increasing number of superficial strategies for school change. The original version of this strategy was developed during our early experience of working with English secondary schools in grappling with the complexities and challenge of large-scale change as part of the school improvement programme we called Improving the Quality of Education for All. The eponymous book (Hopkins 2002b) contains more detail of the approach advocated here. The schools that we worked with believed that much more can be gained for students and staff alike if development work is focused around the *core business of teaching and learning* and *building a capacity for sustained improvement*. While focusing on the learning needs of students in the context of systemic and environmental demands, they also recognized that their improvement strategy must reflect both these demands as well as offering a suitable vehicle for the future development of the school. In this sense the strategy provides the *skeleton* that supports cultural growth, rather than the framework that constrains it.

This three-phase school improvement process has at its core an unrelenting focus on learning and attainment. Given this central focus, the school improvement strategy encompasses both *classroom practice*, particularly the expansion of teacher's teaching repertoire, and the *building of capacity* at the school level, especially the redesign of staff development. While this is not a 'quick-fix' approach, many of the activities involved will bring short as well as medium-term gains. It is also important to note, that although relatively generic, this strategy is not appropriate for failing schools. The approach assumes some limited capacity that unfortunately is too often lacking in those schools.

The three phases are:

- *Phase 1*: Establishing the process, which usually takes up to two terms.
- *Phase 2*: Going whole school, which involves up to a term and a half of work.
- *Phase 3:* Sustaining momentum and networking, when the process has become self-sustaining and internal and external collaboration is the norm.

Phase 1: Establishing the process

Preparing for the strategy involves generating commitment, planning and gathering data on the school level conditions. Although it is important to move into action as soon as is practicable, it is vital that the school improvement group is fully established and has carefully planned the whole-school improvement strategy.

This phase involves:

- commitment to the school improvement approach
- selection of school improvement group
- enquiring into the strengths and weaknesses of the school
- designing the whole-school programme
- seeding the whole-school approach.

The early flow of school improvement activity is illustrated in Figure 6.7.

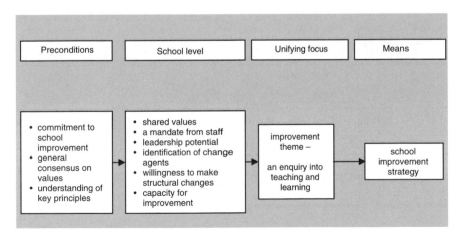

Figure 6.7 Phase 1: Establishing the process

Phase 2: Going whole school

This cycle of activity begins and ends with a whole-staff day. In the first, the curriculum and teaching focus and learning teams will be established. In the second, the staff will share with each other on a curriculum tour around the school the progress they have made.

The activities in this phase are:

- initial whole-school INSET day(s)
- establishing the curriculum and teaching focus
- establishing the learning teams
- initial cycle of enquiry
- sharing initial success and impact on student learning on the curriculum tour.

The flow of activity during this phase of the process is illustrated in Figure 6.8.

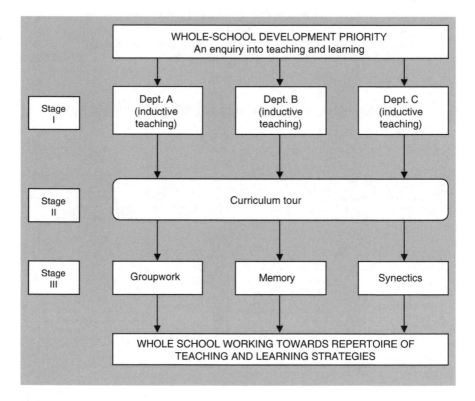

Figure 6.8 Phase 2: Going whole school – the curriculum tour

Phase 3: Sustaining momentum

It is in this phase that the capacity for change at school and classroom level becomes more secure. Learning teams become an established way of working, there is an expansion of the range of teaching strategies used throughout the curriculum and networking with other schools becomes more purposeful.

Activities in this phase of work include:

- establishing further cycles of enquiry
- building teacher learning into the process
- sharpening the focus on student learning
- reflecting on the culture of the school and department
- building networks.

As we developed this approach to school improvement, we built networking into the process. As the number of cohorts of school rolled out, groups of schools increasingly provided support for each other and very soon became self-sustaining. This process is captured in Figure 6.9.

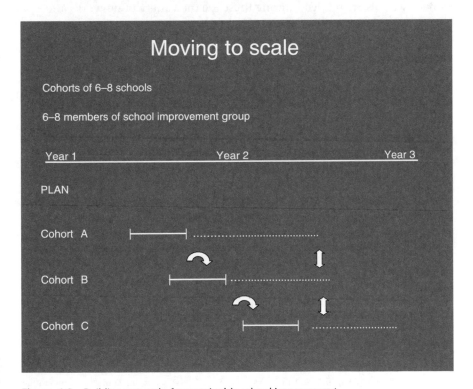

Figure 6.9 Building networks for sustainable school improvement

The virtue of this three-phase process is that, during it, schools realize that effective school improvement is not about choosing from an *à la carte* menu, but rather creating a *comprehensive strategy* that is both systemic and purposeful. As schools develop a 'whole-school' approach, where individual initiatives are linked together in a coherent strategy designed to address the learning needs of student, they begin to want to create networks to share and learn from each other. As has been argued throughout, networks hold the key to the new organization of schooling. So it is to a more extended discussion of networks that we turn in the following section.

Networking for school transformation

During the last decade we became familiar with the emphasis on competition and individual school accountability as drivers for school improvement. These were important strategies for the first phase of a large-scale long-term educational reform programme. As we move into a new phase of educational reform, however, more creative and responsive structures for supporting the work of schools are needed. Among these are the variety of networks and collaborative arrangements schools engage in to support a range of school improvement, professional development and innovative activities. Many argue that networks are the essential unit of organization as we leave behind us the false dichotomy between 'top-down' and 'bottom-up' approaches to educational change.[1] Unfortunately there are various interpretations of the word network; it is a concept open to a high degree of conceptual pluralism. Although many claims are made for the positive impact of networks on school organizational culture and student standards of achievement, in practice, some networks can simply be 'clubs' for sharing 'good practice'. If networks are genuinely to deliver the outcomes claimed for them, we require a far more robust definition of the term and a clearer specification of the processes involved.[2]

Let me therefore propose a definition of the type of network that has a chance of realizing the aspirations the argument so far has for them:

[1] See for example Hargreaves, D.H. (2003b) *Working Laterally: How Innovation Networks Make an Education Epidemic*. London: DfES Publications; Huberman, M. (1995) Networks that alter teaching: conceptualizations, exchanges and experiments, *Teachers and Teaching: Theory and Practice*, 1(2): 193–211.

[2] This section draws in part on a paper prepared for the second phase of the OECD Schooling for Tomorrow programme on educational innovation. The first phase of the programme, including the Hiroshima OECD/Japan conference held at the end of 1997, was focused at the level of the individual institution and culminated in the publication in 1999 of *Innovating Schools*. Since then, the emphasis has broadened to examine innovation through networks, multi-site change and supporting initiatives. Here I also draw on the research evidence on school improvement in general, the recent network experience in England, and the work of the OECD Schooling for Tomorrow programme (see www.oecd.org).

Networks are purposeful social entities characterised by a commitment to quality, rigour, and a focus on standards and student learning. They are also an effective means of supporting innovation in times of change. In education, networks promote the dissemination of good practice, enhance the professional development of teachers, support capacity building in schools, mediate between centralised and decentralised structures, and assist in the process of re-structuring and re-culturing educational organisations and systems.

This definition is admittedly a little dense. In order to amplify the ideas it contains, I will briefly:

- identify a set of conditions necessary to support networks
- outline the role of networks in supporting innovation
- propose an evolving typology of networks.

Conditions necessary for effective networks

The qualities of networks implied by our definition just given are not easily acquired. All the evidence suggests that a number of key conditions need to be in place if networks are to realize their potential as agents of educational innovation. They are:

- *Consistency of values and focus.* It is important that networks have a common aim and purpose and that the values underpinning the network are well articulated and 'owned' by those involved. This consistency of values and purpose also relates to the need for the focus of the network to be unrelentingly on the learning and achievement of students within a socially just education system.
- *Clarity of structure.* Effective networks are well organized with clear operating procedures and mechanisms for ensuring that maximum participation is achieved within and between schools. These structures promote involvement that is broad based, preferably with a whole organization or systemic focus, rather than being narrow, limiting or particular. The clarity of structure also needs to be complemented by an organizational culture that is sceptical about its own rhetoric.
- *Knowledge creation, utilization and transfer.* The key purpose of networks is to create and disseminate knowledge to support educational improvement and innovation. Such knowledge and practice needs to be based on evidence, focus on classroom processes and be available in a form that facilitates teacher learning.
- *Rewards related to learning.* Those who belong to networks need to feel that their involvement is worthwhile. Rewards for networking are best related to supporting professional development and the

encouraging of teacher and student learning. Effective networks invest in people.

- *Dispersed leadership and empowerment.* Highly effective networks contain skilful people who collaborate and work well together. The skills required by network members are similar to the skills sets associated with effective teams and include a focus on dispersed leadership and empowerment.
- *Adequate resources.* Networks need to be adequately resourced, particularly in terms of time, finance and human capital. It is not necessarily the quantum of resource that is important, more crucially there needs to be flexibility in the way in which it is deployed for network purposes.

Role of networks in supporting innovation

Networks can provide a means of facilitating local innovation and change as well as contributing to large-scale reform. They offer the potential for 'reinventing' local support for schools by promoting different forms of collaboration, linkages and multifunctional partnerships. These are sometimes referred to, as earlier, as 'crossover structures'. In this respect, the network enables stakeholders to make connections and to commit to synergistic activity around common priorities. The system emphasis is not to achieve control (which is impossible), but to harness the interactive capability of systemic forces.[3] This analysis also leads to the realization that networks need to be engaged from the very beginnings of a change process, as well as providing support once the process has been established.

To summarize, on the basis of this analysis it is clear that networks have the potential to support educational innovation and change by:

- Keeping the focus on the core purposes of schooling in particular the focus on student learning.
- Enhancing the skill of teachers, leaders and other educators in change agent skills, managing the change process and creating and sustaining a discourse on teaching and learning.
- Providing a focal point for the dissemination of good practice, the generalizability of innovation and the creation of 'action-oriented' knowledge about effective educational practices.
- Building capacity for continuous improvement at a local level, and in particular in creating professional learning communities, within and between schools.

[3] For a further discussion of these points see, Fullan, M. (2000) The return of large-scale reform, *Journal of Educational Change*, 1(1): 1–23.

- Ensuring that systems of pressure and support are *integrated*, not segmented. For example, professional learning communities incorporate pressure and support in a seamless way.
- Acting as a link between the centralized and decentralized schism resulting from many contemporary policy initiatives. In particular, in contributing to policy coherence horizontally and vertically.

Towards a typology of networks

It is evident that in the context of supporting innovation one can discern the beginnings of a typology of networks. At the basic level, networks facilitate the sharing of good practice, at the highest level, they can act as agents of system renewal. Briefly, the emerging typology of networks is as follows:

1   At its most basic level, a network could be regarded as simply groups of teachers joining together for a common curriculum purpose and for the sharing of good practice.
2   At a more ambitious level, networks could involve groups of teachers and schools joining together for the purposes of school improvement with the explicit aim of not just sharing practice, but of enhancing teaching, learning and student achievement throughout a school or groups of schools.
3   Over and above this, networks could also not just serve the purpose of knowledge transfer and school improvement, but also involve groups of stakeholders joining together for the implementation of specific policies locally and possibly nationally.
4   A further extension of this way of working is found when groups of networks (within and outside education) link together for system improvement in terms of social justice and inclusion.
5   Finally, there is the potential for groups of networks to work together, not just on a social justice agenda, but also to act explicitly as agents for system renewal and transformation.

This typology not only provides a way of categorizing networks, but also demonstrates how they have an explicit role to play in systemic change. If we refer again to the 'segments' diagram, one can see that the first level of networking describes the common approach in the left-hand segment; levels two and three loosely describe practice within the middle segment; and levels four and five begin to capture aspects of the new educational landscape imagined by the right-hand segment. At present this is by no means an exact science, but the progression implied by the typology maps well onto the direction of travel that was argued for in Chapter 2.

Another way of describing this progression is by thinking about networks according to purpose. This allows us to think beyond specific programmes or initiatives and to reconsider the current network landscape in the light of their ability to transform that landscape. Figure 6.10, which is based on work done by the DfES' Innovation Unit, suggests three key purposes for networks. They all reflect different approaches to enhancing student outcomes and seem to represent the breadth of network activity *currently* taking place. The diagram, as we shall see, can also be used as a way of thinking about and describing future networks.

We begin by taking the purposes of each in turn:

Enhancing the curriculum offer to learners

A network formed for this purpose is based on an understanding that to deliver a more personalized learning programme to students, schools have to work together. These networks of schools, probably with other partners, have the potential to respond creatively to serving the 'whole' learner. Charles Leadbeater (2004) has argued that the schools in this kind of network could act as 'solutions assemblers', whereby individual institutions see themselves as gateways to a flexible network of provision.

Accelerating improvement and stimulating innovation

Over time, a network with this as their initial focus can provide a focal point for the distribution of good practice. For teachers, being part of the network provides opportunities to create, validate and spread knowledge

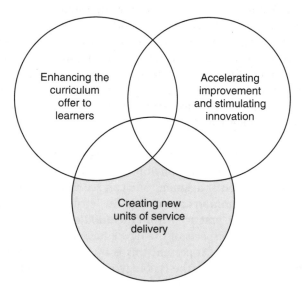

Figure 6.10   Three key purposes for networks

about what works beyond the boundaries of individual classrooms and schools. Such networks build capacity for continuous improvement at the local level by creating professional learning communities within and between schools (Wenger 1998). Collaboration facilitates a shift towards a culture that embraces openness, support and trust in testing new solutions.

Creating new units of service delivery

These networks allow the traditional boundaries between schools to be eroded and, instead, schools work in close partnership to take responsibility for all their children. As much as the current system allows, there is a commitment to being held to mutual account and simplifying structures that have previously underlined institutional parameters. This is particularly relevant to the momentum behind establishing schools as social centres. In England this movement is reflected in the establishing of the 'extended' (full-service) school and children's trusts (as the commissioner of services for children including education).

It should now be easy to see how, as these purposes begin to overlap, the network begins to move from the left-hand side of the original diagram to the right. Complete overlap between these three core purposes delivers not only the scenario implied by levels 4 and 5 of the typology, but also the right-hand segment of the diagram where schools lead reform and every school is or is becoming great. Looking at current practice in England, one can see some of the existing network initiatives beginning to combine some of these three purposes. Those networks formed through the Leading Edge Partnership programme, for example, would probably articulate their primary purpose as being close to that of accelerating improvement and stimulating innovation. The third of the purposes, which covers governance and accountability, will resonate with groups of schools that have become federations. Each of these groups of schools are now beginning to assume the purposes of the other. Many of our leading schools are becoming more ambitious for themselves and the system as a whole and as a consequence are deliberately integrating the three purposes outlined in the diagram. As they do, they are self-consciously recreating the landscape of education and giving us some glimpses into what the right-hand segment of the diagram could look like.

It is also pleasing to see the positive impact of networking on student learning. The recent external evaluation of the National College of School Leaders Networked Learning Communities programme for example (Earl et al. 2006) suggests that when networks of schools work together, there is an impact on pupil learning. The number of people in the school who are active in the network was positively correlated with pupil outcomes in English, maths and science at Key Stage 2 and value-added scores at Key Stage 3. The factor 'overall network influence' was positively correlated with GCSE change score and the level of network attachment was related to changes in pupil outcomes in maths and science at Key Stage 3. Network attachment was also correlated with the intermediate outcome of changes in thinking and practice in schools.

In light of this, there is a danger that in talking about structures and governance we may overly reify networks and begin to fall into the trap of seeing them as ends rather than as means. In making the link between this and the final section, let me reiterate that networks are needed principally to spread best practice and ensure that improvement is generated across the system. Networks of schools provide the capacity (i) to discipline and transfer innovation and (ii) to create a cultural willingness within the profession to re-examine existing practice so as to ensure consistency and tackle within-school variation. In the final section of this chapter we will take a brief look at innovation. It complements the discussion of viral ways of working as an alternative approach to educational change in Chapter 1.

Coda: innovation and viral ways of working

In his monograph The *Education Epidemic* (2003a) David Hargreaves not only described the various forms of capital as they applied to schools, but also outlined an agenda for educational transformation based on innovation and networking. The essential task, Hargreaves argued, is to create a climate in which it is possible for teachers to actively engage in innovation and to transfer validated innovations rapidly within their school and into other schools. This does not mean a return to 'letting a thousand flowers bloom', but a disciplined approach to innovation.

If leading-edge schools – by definition a minority – take the lead in knowledge creation he asks, what happens to innovation in the rest of the system? Hargreaves responds that transformation is achieved in two ways:

- by moving the best schools (or departments within them) further ahead. That is, through *frontline innovation* conducted by leading-edge institutions and government-supported 'pathfinders', which develop new ideas into original practices
- by closing the gap between the least and most effective schools (or subject departments) – *transferred innovation*.

Transformation thus combines 'moving ahead' with 'levelling up'.

To achieve such a 'lateral strategy' for transferred innovation requires the following strategic components:

- it must become clear what is meant by 'good' and 'best' practice among teachers

- there needs to be a method of locating good practice and sound innovations
- innovations must be ones that bring real advantages to teachers
- methods of transferring innovation effectively have to be devised.

Networks, Hargreaves argued, are the foundations for an innovative system of education. Only networks can deliver a mix of vertical-central and lateral-local reform strategies necessary for transformation. In short, the system itself has to become a more self-conscious and effective learning system in parallel to the learning organization advocated for schools. This is the issue we address in the final part of the book.

PART 3
Realizing the system leadership dividend

The key to every school's being a great school is the way in which leadership moulds the four drivers to context and produces organizations capable of sustained improvement. Additionally, the way in which schools at different phases of the performance cycle support one another demonstrates how leadership can help move the system from one of national prescription to one where professionalism provides the energy and force for sustainability. The concept to system leadership is outlined in this final part and there is a further discussion of how this movement can go to scale.

7   The power of system leadership

To achieve an educational system where every school has a chance of becoming great and where personalized learning is the norm, a rebalancing between national prescription and schools leading reform with a presumption towards the latter is required. In making the transition from 'prescription' to 'professionalism', strategies are required that not only continue to raise standards but also build capacity within the system. The argument has been that the four drivers described in the previous chapters, if pursued relentlessly and deeply, have the potential to deliver 'every school a great school'. Although these key trends provide a core strategy for improvement, the argument being made in this book is that it is system leadership that moulds them to context. This is seen in the 'diamond of reform' in Figure 7.1, where the four drivers coalesce through the exercise of responsible system leadership.

It is the power of system leaders to adapt the four drivers to particular and individual school contexts. It is leadership that enables systemic reform to be both generic in terms of overall strategy and specific in adapting to individual and particular situations. It is also system leaders who reach beyond their own school to create networks and collaborative arrangements that not only add richness and excellence to the learning of students, but also act as we saw in the previous chapter, as agents of educational transformation.

This thought is also caught by Michael Fullan (2004) in his book *Leadership and Sustainability* in the following way:

> *You can't develop systems directly. You have to use the system to develop itself. Again, we have high-yield strategy. Invest a little to help leaders to lead beyond their schools, and reap the benefit.*
>
> *Some forms of lateral capacity building occur within the school or within the district. These are the responsibility of school and district leaders. System leaders can establish explicit expectations that these kinds of intra-organizational, professional-learning communities are deep and valuable.*

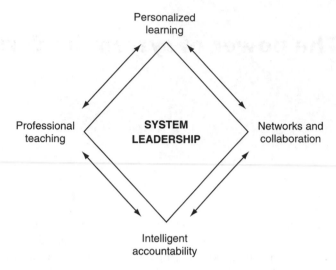

Figure 7.1 System leadership moulds the key drivers to context

> *Beyond this, system leaders have a special responsibility to foster and support cross-system networks, where people across a region, state, or country learn from each other. When done well, this had multiple payoffs for our system sustainability agenda. First, people get access to good ideas from other practitioners – ideas that are grounded and workable from respected peers who have successfully grappled with difficult problems. Second, people begin to identify with larger parts of the system beyond their narrow interest groups. We have seen in time and again in our work. When people get out to do something worthwhile with peers in other schools or jurisdictions, the sense of community and commitment enlarges. One's identity to a larger common purpose amplifies. Third, if enough people get out where 'system concerns' form the substance of the exchanges – the collective capacity to system think, and thus to system change, if advanced.*

Fullan describes well the contribution that system leaders can make to educational transformation, but there is a complicating factor here. Although each of these four drivers is integral to a social democratic settlement for education, their system-wide impact is both complicated and facilitated by the high degree of differentiation within most school systems. Yet, system transformation depends on excellent practice being developed, shared, demonstrated and adopted across and between schools.

So, in the move towards ensuring that every school is a great school, the four drivers provide a necessary, but not sufficient condition. The missing ingredient is the concept of *segmentation*. The key idea being that all schools are at different stages in their improvement cycle, on a continuum from 'failing' to 'leading'. This opens up the possibility of a highly differentiated approach to school improvement given that different schools will both need, and be able to provide, different forms of support and intervention at different times.

So, before describing in detail the concept of system leadership one has to confront the necessary challenge of differentiation in school systems. This chapter is eventually in two sections. The first section, which develops the concept of segmentation, will:

- briefly review the concept of differential school improvement
- discuss the proposition that segmentation is the key to every school being a great school.

The second section is devoted to the 'power of system leadership' and will:

- propose a definition and elaborate the concept of system leadership
- review the evidence of the effectiveness of system leaders in turning around failing schools
- conclude by proposing a model for system leadership that incorporates 'a theory of action'.

Differential school improvement

In *School Improvement for Real*,[1] I rehearsed the well-evidenced argument that the research on school effectiveness is unequivocal that schools are differentially effective.[2] I then began to suggest that this finding must lead to the conclusion that schools at different levels of effectiveness require different strategies for school improvement. I then continued to speculate that strategies for school development need to fit the 'growth state' or culture of the particular school, and the corollary that strategies effective for improving performance at one 'growth state' are not necessarily effective at another. I then outlined a framework to organize thinking around this issue, as seen in Figure 7.2.

The diagonal (regression) line represents the level of achievement one would expect from a student based on their prior attainment on entry to a school, having controlled for background variables. Datasets from national LEA and school district studies, where such individual student scores are

[1] See Chapter 9 in Hopkins, D. (2001) *School Improvement for Real*. London: Routledge/Falmer.
[2] See for example Teddlie, C. and Reynolds, D. (2000) *The International Handbook of School Effectiveness Research*. London: Falmer Press.

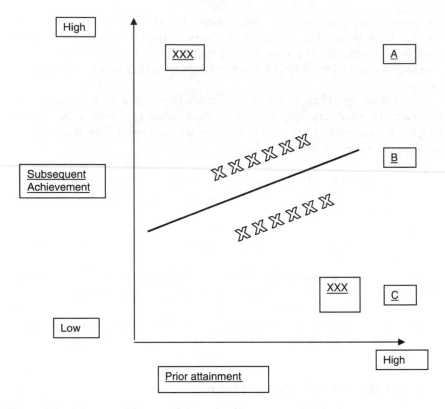

Figure 7.2 A framework for considering school improvement strategies

available, suggest that on average most schools cluster around the line, as in B on the diagram. These datasets sometimes contain a few schools, such as those at A, which consistently 'add value' to their students in comparison with what one would expect from measures of these students' prior attainment. Unfortunately, these datasets occasionally also contain schools, such as those at C, that consistently reduce the levels of student achievement one would expect.

What is of central importance for those interested in every school becoming great, is not just what the capacities of schools at A, B and C are, but how do schools at C assume the characteristics of those schools at A, and what strategies can be used to help them do this? Although the research base on the effects of school improvement strategies is weak, it is sensible to assume that the same strategy will not move a school directly from C to A, and that a strategy for moving a school from position C to position B would be qualitatively different from a strategy that would move a school from position B to position A. It would also make sense to assume that a strategy that helps to keep a school at A is different again.

Further support for this point of view is found in our *Improving Schools* study (Gray et al. 1999). The research explored how schools became effective over time and we identified three different 'routes to improvement'.

Tactics

A tactical response to improvement was evident in all of the schools involved in the research. These initiatives or tactics included: monitoring performance, targeting students, introducing extra classes for certain groups of students, implementing 'codes of conduct', giving students greater responsibility, changing examination boards and so on. They comprise the 'common curriculum' of school improvement. This combination of tactics is powerful enough to raise the performance of low or slowly achieving schools up towards the (regression) line, but no further. The data suggested a plateau effect after, at best, a couple of years.

Strategies

There was another group of schools in the sample that seemed to be able to do more and progress further than those that only responded to the challenge of school improvement tactically. Schools that acted strategically employed the tactical responses, but with two major differences. First, the school's staff were all engaged in a coordinated response to the challenge of school improvement. The leadership of the school and many of the staff were not content with just doing something; they wanted to do it with a purpose. Second, the focus of their work was explicitly at the classroom or 'learning' level. Serious efforts were being made in these schools to coordinate and deliver a whole-school response – to ensure some consistency of practice from one department to another. What was striking in these schools, and clearly differentiated them from schools that employed a tactical response, was that they were clearly interested in the dynamics of student learning and classroom practice.

Capacities (for further improvement)

There are also schools that regularly transcend the strategic improvement dimension. These are schools that are already at relatively high levels of effectiveness and build on this by employing a far more sophisticated approach to change. These are schools that collectively understand the causes of positive change and the areas of resistance in the school. They know when change is happening and understand the reasons why, and are able to find ways to sustain positive change into the medium and long term. (These schools are responsive to what Ron Heifetz (1994) called *adaptive challenges*, a concept we will be discussing later in this chapter.) Above all, they have developed a willingness to go beyond the incremental approach to restructuring and genuinely see school improvement as a way of life.

Our current research into school improvement and system leadership is focusing on the dynamics of improvement in schools that employ this more strategic and capacity building approach. There seem to be nine components that need to be worked on at the same time in order to ensure that the most effective conditions are in place to personalize learning. These are in no particular order:

1   *Teaching and learning: are consistently good.* Classroom ethos of high expectations, shared 'good lesson' structure, high proportion of time on task, good use of AfL to plan lessons and tailor to need.

2   *Curriculum: is balanced and interesting.* Strategic planning to integrate basics, breadth and cognitive learning, with KS3 interventions in basic skills, grade enhancement classes and mentoring.

3   *Behaviour: promotes order and enjoyment.* Consistent rules for conduct and dress, with consistent implications for infringement consistently applied.

4   *Student attitudes to learning.* Attendance is high, pastoral care is accessible, achievement is acknowledged, students have a voice in school decision making.

5   *Leadership.* Clear vision is translated into manageable, time bound and agreed objectives, commitment is established, data are used to tackle weaknesses and internal variation.

6   *Professional learning community.* Dedicated time for a range of CPD opportunities to share experience of improving practice, with focus on identifying individual need especially for weak/poor teaching.

7   *Internal accountability: 'empowers through a culture of discipline'.* Agreed expectations for teaching quality and quality assurance and peer observation.

8   *Resources and environmental management: is student focused.* Use of funding streams, whole-school team approach and the environment all support learning.

9   *Partnerships beyond the school: creating learning opportunities.* Parental engagement is encouraged and support agencies are used effectively.

All nine points link together to create a distinctive school culture as seen in Figure 7.3.

The critical issue, however, is not the identification of the nine components, the importance of which is nowadays well understood, but how they interact and develop within particular school settings. There seem to be four dimensions to the process:

Strategy for improvement

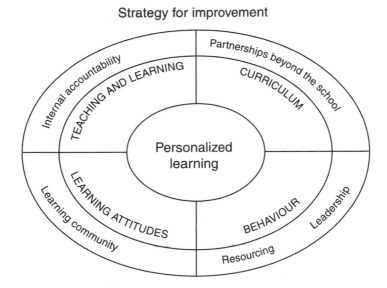

Figure 7.3 The nine components for strategic school improvement

- *Generating the improvement narrative.* A clear reform narrative is created and seen by staff to be consistently applied, with a vision and urgency that translates into clear principles for action.
- *Organizing the key strategies.* Improvement activities are selected and linked together strategically, supported by robust and highly reliable school management teams' (SMTs) roles in key areas.
- *Professional learning at the heart of the process.* Improvement strategy informs CPD; knowledge is gained, verified and refined by staff to underpin improvement; networking is used to manage risk and discipline practice.
- *Cultures are subsequently changed and developed.* Professional ethos and values that support capacity building are initiated, implemented and institutionalized, so that a culture of disciplined action replaces excessive control.

The process of school development outlined in the previous chapter illustrates one of the ways schools are linking these four elements together in an overall strategy for sustained improvement.

The purpose of this section has (a) been to focus on the importance of acknowledging the need for differential school improvement strategies and (b) to give some indication of the complexities involved. Bearing this essentially school-level discussion in mind, we can turn in the following section to an analysis of how this plays out at a system level.

Segmentation as the key to 'every school a great school'

One of the challenges to realizing 'every school a great school' and the reason why reform efforts struggle to achieve a system-wide impact is because change is complicated by the high degree of segmentation within the school system. There are, as we have seen, large groups of schools at varying stages of the performance cycle between low and high performing. For every school to be great, we need to move to a new trajectory through using this diversity to drive higher levels of performance throughout the system. System transformation depends on excellent practice being developed, shared, demonstrated and adopted across and between schools.

It is important to realize, however, that this aspiration of system transformation being facilitated by the degree of segmentation existing in the system only holds when certain conditions are in place. There are two crucial aspects to this:

- First, that there is increased clarity on the nature of intervention and support for schools at each phase of the performance cycle.
- Second, that schools at each phase are clear as to the most productive ways in which to collaborate in order to capitalize on the diversity within the system.

In both cases it is clear that one size does not fit all.

The following discussion reflects experience in the English secondary school system, but as before, the analysis is designed to have a more general applicability. In appreciating that the current secondary school system is highly segmented there is a delicate balance to be achieved between empirical precision and operational clarity. Building on the initial discussion an overview of the relative performance of English secondary schools is found in Figure 7.4.

Based on this type of analysis, there are probably six clearly identifiable levels of performance within the current structure of the English secondary school that are recognized by both statisticians and those tasked with improving schools. These six school types, when taken together, comprise the full range of the secondary school performance cycle. They, together with their key strategies for improvement, are:

Leading schools

Possibly 10% of secondary schools. These are the highest performing schools that also have the capacity to lead others. Their route to further improvement and contribution to the system comes in at least two forms: first, becoming

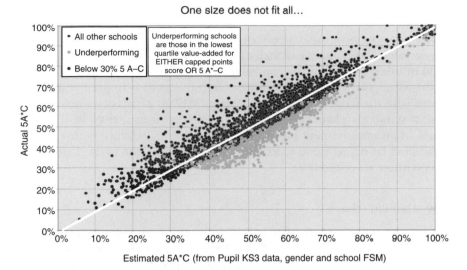

Figure 7.4   An overview of the relative performance of English secondary schools

leading practitioners through disseminating best practice and networking; and, second, through working more formally and systematically with lower performing schools through some 'federation' arrangement to improve the partner school's performance.

Succeeding, self-improving schools

Possibly 20% of secondary schools. These are schools that have consistently above average levels of value-added and that exhibit aspects of best practice that will benefit the system through further dissemination. Their route to further improvement and contribution to the system comes in networking their best practice in local networks using their leading teachers to mentor in other schools and to take students from local schools into their areas of specialism.

Succeeding schools with significant areas of underperformance

Possibly 20% of secondary schools. These schools, although successful on published criteria, have unacceptable numbers of underperforming teachers or departments who are masked by the averaging out of published results. Their route to further improvement and contribution to the system comes, on the one hand, contributing as earlier to other schools from their areas of strength and being, on the other, the recipients of such support in their weaker areas.

Underperforming schools

Possibly 25% of secondary schools. Defined as those secondary schools in their lowest value-added quartile of their distribution, which may have adequate or good headline results, but are consistently failing to add value to the progress of their students. Their route to further improvement is to use the data discussed with the school improvement partner (SIP) as a basis of a whole-school raising standards plan. They will need sustained consultancy in the early stages of an improvement process from a school (or schools) with a similar intake, but far higher value-added using a modified version of the 'federations intervention' described later.

Low-attaining schools

Possibly 20% of secondary schools. Defined as those secondary schools below the 30% A*–C GCSE floor target but with a capacity to improve. Their route to further improvement requires sustained support through some federation arrangement or involvement, consultancy support through the national strategies and possibly the application of an improvement grant.

Failing schools

Possibly 5% of secondary schools. Defined as being well below the floor target and with little capacity to improve. At a minimum, these schools will require intervention in the form of a 'hard federation' or membership of the intensive support programme. If these strategies are not successful in the short term, then closure, academy status or a school's competition is the only other answer in order to sustain adequate provision for the students involved.

A summary of this approach is set out in Table 7.1. In the right-hand column is a basic taxonomy of schools based on an analysis of secondary schools in England. The number of categories and the terminology will vary from setting to setting, the crucial point being is that not all schools are the same and each requires different forms of support. This is the focus of the second column, where a range of strategies for supporting schools at different phases of their development are briefly described. Again these descriptions are grounded in the English context, but they do have a more universal applicability. There are two key points here:

- The first is that, as we have just seen, one size does not fit all.
- The second is that these different forms of intervention and support are increasingly being provided by schools themselves, rather than being imposed and delivered by some external agency. This approach

Table 7.1 The six types of English secondary school and their key strategies for improvement

Type of school	Key strategies – responsive to context and need
Leading schools	• Become leading practitioners • Formal federation with lower performing schools
Succeeding, self-improving schools	• Regular local networking for school leaders • Between-school curriculum development
Succeeding schools with internal variations	• Consistency interventions: such as assessment for learning • Subject specialist support to particular departments
Underperforming schools	• Linked school support for underperforming departments • Underperforming pupil programmes: catch-up
Low attaining schools	• Formal support in federation structure • Consultancy in core subjects and best practice
Failing schools	• Intensive support programme • New provider such as an academy

to system transformation relies fundamentally on school to school support as the basis of the improvement strategy.

However, in order to be successful the segmentation approach requires a fair degree of boldness in setting system level expectations and conditions. There are four implications in particular that have to be grappled with:

- All failing and underperforming (and potentially low-achieving) schools should have a leading school that works with them in either a formal grouping federation (where the leading school principal or head assumes overall control and accountability) or in more informal partnership. Evidence from research I conducted with Rob Higham for the National College for School Leadership on existing School Federations in England suggested that, a national system of federations would be capable of delivering a sustainable step change in improvement in relatively short periods of time (Higham and Hopkins 2005). For example a number of 'federated schools,' as is seen later, have improved their 5 A*–Cs at GCSE from under 20% to over 50% in two years.
- Schools should take greater responsibility for neighbouring schools, so that the move towards networking encourages groups of schools to form collaborative arrangements outside of local control. This would be on the condition that these schools provide extended services for

all students within a geographic area, but equally on the acceptance that there would be incentives for doing so. Encouraging local schools to work together will build capacity for continuous improvement at local level.

- The incentives for greater system responsibility should include significantly enhanced funding for students most at risk. Beyond incentivizing local collaboratives, the potential effects for large-scale long-term reform include:
  - a more even distribution of 'at risk' students and associated increases in standards, due to more schools seeking to admit a larger proportion of 'at risk' students so as to increase their overall income
  - a significant reduction in 'sink schools' even where 'at risk' students are concentrated, as there would be much greater potential to respond to the socio economic challenges (for example by paying more to attract the best teachers or by developing excellent parental involvement and outreach services).
- A rationalization of national and local agency functions and roles to allow the higher degree of national and regional coordination for this increasingly devolved system.

These proposals extend the discussion in the previous chapter on networking, but are consistent with the direction in which those recommendations were taking us. These current proposals also have a combination of school- and policy-level implications. This is consistent with the phase of adaptive change the overall system is currently in. If we are to move towards a system based on informed professional judgement, then capacity has to be simultaneously built at the school and system level as both schools and government learn new ways of working, establish new norms of engagement and build more flexible and problem-oriented work cultures.

But still, there is a missing ingredient – the necessity for outstanding leadership as the system as a whole grapples with the challenge of adaptive change. As we shall see in the next section, it is system leadership that has the power to maximize the impact of both the four drivers and the energy of segmentation and make them work in different contexts.

System leadership as the catalyst for systemic change

I have argued that it is leadership that shapes the drivers to context, but this is obviously not a form of leadership that is commonplace. Traditional leadership and management approaches are well able to accommodate technical problems. The future, however, is about solving problems for which there is no immediate solution and then to build the capacity for doing this into the medium and long term. This requires leadership of a different order.

The literature on leadership has mushroomed in recent years as have leadership courses and qualifications. All seem to have a slightly different take on leadership and claims on truth, which I for one find a little confusing. In this section, I will set out an approach to leadership, which I am calling 'system leadership', that accommodates the arguments for sustainable educational transformation made in the preceding pages.

'System leaders' are those head teachers who are willing to shoulder system leadership roles: who care about and work for the success of other schools as well as their own. In England, there appears to be an emerging cadre of these head teachers, who stand in contrast to the competitive ethic of headship so prevalent in the 1990s. It is these educators, who, by their own efforts and commitment, are beginning to transform the nature of leadership and educational improvement in this country. Interestingly, there is also evidence of this role emerging in other leading educational systems in Europe, North America and Australia (Hopkins forthcoming).

In terms of the argument here, this leads me to a simple proposition:

> *If our goal is 'every school a great school', then policy and practice has to focus on system improvement. This means that a school head has to be almost as concerned about the success of other schools, as he or she is about his or her own school. Sustained improvement of schools is not possible unless the whole system is moving forward.*

Our recent research on system leadership began to map the system leadership landscape (Hopkins and Higham forthcoming). It identified a significant amount of system leadership activity in England, far more than previously expected. However, we are still in the process of charting the system leadership movement, as we work inductively from the behaviours of the outstanding leaders we are privileged to collaborate with. From all these evidence we can provide a sketch of some of the key aspects of the role:

- moral purpose of system leadership
- system leadership roles
- system leadership as adaptive work
- the domains of system leadership.

The first thing to say is that system leadership, as Michael Fullan (2003, 2005) has argued, is imbued with *moral purpose*. Without that, there would not be the passion to proceed or the encouragement for others to follow. In England, for example, where the regularities of improvement in teaching and learning are still not well understood, where deprivation is still too good a predictor of educational success and where the goal is for every school to be a great school, the leadership challenge is surely a systemic one. This perspective gives a broader appreciation of what is meant by the moral purpose of system leadership.

I would argue, therefore, that system leaders express their moral purpose through:

1   measuring their success in terms of improving student learning and increasing achievement and strive to both raise the bar and narrow the gap(s)

2   being fundamentally committed to the improvement of teaching and learning. They engage deeply with the organization of teaching, learning, curriculum and assessment in order to ensure that learning is personalized for all their students

3   developing their schools as personal and professional learning communities, with relationships built across and beyond each school to provide a range of learning experiences and professional development opportunities

4   striving for equity and inclusion through acting on context and culture. This is not just about eradicating poverty, as important as that is – it is also about giving communities a sense of worth and empowerment

5   realizing in a deep way that the classroom, school and system levels all impact on one another. Crucially, they understand that in order to change the larger system you have to engage with it in a meaningful way.

Although this degree of clarity is not necessarily obvious in the behaviour and practice of every head teacher, these aspirations are increasingly becoming part of the conventional wisdom of the best of our global educational leaders.

Second, it is also pleasing to see a variety of *system leader roles* emerging within various systems that are consistent with such a moral purpose. At present, in England, these are (Hopkins and Higham forthcoming):

- Developing and *leading a successful educational improvement partnership*[3] between several schools, often focused on a set of specific themes that have significant and clear outcomes that reach beyond the capacity of any one single institution. These include partnerships on: curriculum design and specialisms, including sharing curricular innovation to respond to key challenges; 14–19 consortia; behaviour

---

[3] This category includes but is not restricted to the more fomalized educational improvement partnerships as defined by the DfES (2005).

and hard to place students. While many such partnerships currently remain in what is commonly referred to as 'soft' organizational collaboratives, some have moved to 'harder' more fomalized arrangements in the form of (co)federations (to develop stronger mechanisms for joint governance and accountability) or education improvement partnerships (to formalize the devolution of certain defined delivery responsibilities and resources from their local authority).

- Choosing to *lead and improve a school in extremely challenging circumstances* and change local contexts by building a culture of success and then sustaining once low-achieving schools as high-valued-added institutions.
- *Partnering another school facing difficulties and improve it*, either as an executive head of a federation or as the leader of a more informal improvement arrangement. Such system leadership is differentiated from category 1 on the basis that leaders here work from a lead school into a low-achieving or underperforming school (or schools) that require intervention. As evidenced by our earlier research on executive heads for the NCSL and the college's subsequent advice on complex schools to the Secretary of State: 'There is a growing body of well-documented evidence from around the country that, where a school is in serious trouble, the use of an executive head teacher/ partner head teacher and a paired arrangement with that head's successful school, can be a particularly effective solution, and is being increasingly widely applied' (NCSL 2005: 3).
- Acting as a *community leader* to broker and shape partnerships and/or networks of wider relationships across local communities to support children's welfare and potential, often through multi-agency work. Such system leadership is rooted firmly within the context of the national ECM and children agendas and responds to, as Osbourne (2000) puts it: 'The acceptance [that] some . . . issues are so complex and interconnected that they require the energy of a number of organizations to resolve and hence can only be tackled through organizations working together' (p.1). And further: 'The concept of [a] full-service school where a range of public and private sector services is located at or near the school is one manifestation' (p.188).
- Working as a *change agent* or expert leader within the system, identifying best classroom practice and transferring it to support improvement in others schools. This is the widest category and includes:
  - heads working as mentor leaders within networks of schools, combining an aspiration and motivation for other schools to improve with the practical knowledge and guidance for them to do so
  - heads who are active and effective leaders within more centrally

organized system leadership programmes, for instance within the consultant leader programme, school improvement partners (SIP) and national leaders of education (NLE)

- heads who with their staff purposely develop exemplary curricula and teaching programmes either for particular groups of students or to develop specific learning outcomes in a form that is transferable to other schools and settings.

These roles could be divided into formal roles that are developed through national programmes and have clear protocols set out in their guidance (for instance: consultant leaders; SIPs; NLEs such as curriculum and pedagogy innovators); and informal that are locally developed and are far more fluid, ad hoc and organic. However, this flexibility is often an important part of how these system leadership roles have come about.

The formal and informal roles hold a very significant potential to effect systemic educational improvement. If a sufficient cadre of system leaders were developed and deployed, there would be:

- a wider resource for school improvement: making the most of our leaders to transfer best practice and reduce the risk of innovation and change focused on attainment and welfare
- an authentic response to failing schools (often those least able to attract suitable leaders)
- a means to resolve the emerging challenge of, on the one hand, falling student rolls and hence increasingly non-viable schools and, on the other hand, pressures to sustain educational provision in all localities
- a sustainable strategy for retaining and developing headteachers as a response to the shortage we are currently facing. A recent survey by the General Teaching Council (2006) warned that 40% of headteacher posts will be filled only with difficulty in the coming years.

No doubt these roles will expand and mature over time; but what is significant about them is that they have evolved in response to the *adaptive challenge of system change*. This is the third of the aspects we need to discuss. As mention earlier in the chapter, it was Ron Heifetz (1994) who focused attention on the concept of an adaptive challenge. An adaptive challenge is a problem situation for which solutions lie outside current ways of operating. This is in stark contrast to a technical problem for which the know-how already exists. This distinction has resonance for educational reform. Put simply, resolving a technical problem is a management issue; tackling adaptive challenges, however, requires leadership. Often, we try to solve technical problems with adaptive processes or more commonly force technical solutions onto adaptive problems. Figure 7.5 captures this distinction and illustrates how this issue underpins the policy conundrum of making the transition from prescription to professionalism and emphasizes the importance of capacity building.

Almost by definition, adaptive challenges demand learning, as progress here requires new ways of thinking and operating. In these instances, it is 'people who are the problem', because an effective response to an adaptive challenge is almost always beyond the current competence of those involved. Inevitably, this is threatening and often the prospect of adaptive work generates heat and resistance.

Mobilizing people to meet adaptive challenges is at the heart of leadership practice. In the short term, leadership helps people meet an immediate challenge. In the medium to long term, leadership generates capacity to enable people to meet an ongoing stream of adaptive challenges. Ultimately, adaptive work requires us to reflect on the moral purpose by which we seek to thrive and demands diagnostic enquiry into the realities we face that threaten the realization of those purposes.

The fourth issue is what are the *domains of system leadership*, what does the task involve? One of the clearest definitions is the four core functions proposed by Ken Leithwood and his colleagues (forthcoming). These are:

- *Setting direction*: to enable every learner to reach their potential and to translate this vision into whole school curriculum, consistency and high expectations.

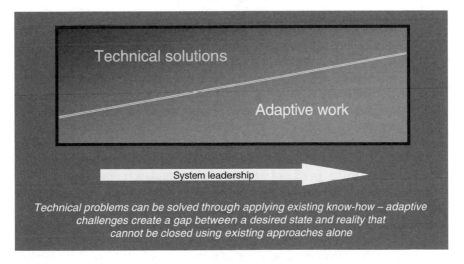

Figure 7.5 System leadership as adaptive work

- *Managing teaching and learning*: to ensure that there is both a high degree of consistency and innovation in teaching practices to enable personalized learning for all students.
- *Developing people*: to enable students to become active learners and to create schools as professional learning communities for teachers.
- *Developing the organization*: to create evidence-based schools and effective organizations and to be involved in networks collaborating to build curriculum diversity, professional support and extended services.

This outline stands up well when it is tested against existing approaches to school leadership that have had a demonstrable impact on student learning. Take for instance, Richard Elmore's (2004: 66) definition of the leadership purpose:

> *Improvement, then, is change with direction, sustained over time, that moves entire systems, raising the average level of quality and performance while at the same time decreasing the variation among units, and engaging people in analysis and understanding of why some actions seem to work and others don't.*
>
> *Leadership is the guidance and direction of instructional improvement. This is a deliberately de-romanticised, focussed and instrumental definition.*

This definition of leadership underpins Elmore's (2004: 68) further contention that 'the purpose of leadership is the improvement of instructional practice and performance' and its four dimensions:

- instructional improvement requires continuous learning
- learning requires modelling
- the roles and activities of leadership flow from the expertise required for learning and improvement, and not from the formal dictates of the institution
- the exercise of authority requires reciprocity of accountability and capacity.

From this analysis, Elmore (2004: 80–81) distils some guiding principles that can be used to design school structures and stimulate training programmes that can result in large-scale improvement. These principles are summarized in Table 7.2. It is also interesting to note that Elmore enters a caveat that is much in tune with the values underpinning this book. He says that:

> *... [The] exact form or wording of the principles is less important than the fact that they are an attempt to derive general guidance from practice*

Table 7.2 Elmore's principles for large-scale improvement

Maintain a tight instructional focus sustained over time
- Apply the instructional focus to everyone in the organization
- Apply it to both practice and performance
- Apply it to a limited number of instructional areas and practices, becoming progressively more ambitious over time

Routinize accountability for practice and performance in face-to-face relationships
- Create a strong normative environment in which adults take responsibility for the academic performance of children
- Rely more heavily on face-to-face relationships than on bureaucratic routines
- Evaluate performance on the basis of all students, not select groups of students and – above all – not school- or grade-level averages
- Design everyone's work primarily in terms of improving the capacity and performance of someone else – system administrators of principals and teachers, principals of teachers, teachers of students. In a well-developed system, the order should be reversed as well

Reduce isolation and open practice up to direct observation, analysis and criticism
- Make direct observation of practice, analysis and feedback a routine feature of work
- Move people across settings, including outsiders into schools
- Centre group discussions on the instructional work of the organization
- Model desired classroom practice in administrative actions
- Model desired classroom practice in collegial interactions

Exercise differential treatment based on performance and capacity,
not on volunteerism
- Acknowledge differences among communities, schools and classrooms within a common framework of improvement
- Allocate supervisory time and professional development based on explicit judgements about where schools are in developmental process of practice and performance

Devolve increased discretion based on practice and performance
- Do not rely on generalized rules about centralization and decentralization
- Loosen and tighten administrative control based on hard evidence of quality of practice and performance of diverse groups of students; greater discretion follows higher quality of practice and higher levels of performance

> and research in a form can be tried in multiple settings and revised and elaborated with experience.

This is a sentiment with which I fully concur.

My own work with schools in England represents a similar logic to school improvement and reflects the argument developed in the last few chapters. This, as Elmore has proposed, is the crucial domain of system leadership. Figure 7.6 contains an illustration of the activities that contribute to a capacity

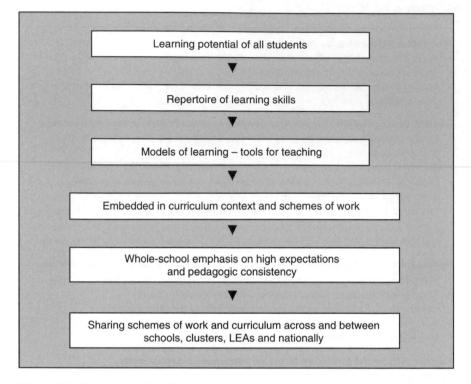

Figure 7.6 The logic of school improvement

for learning within a school and that are facilitated, established and energized by system leaders. It represents an attempt to capture how schools establish a 'learning focus' and how a number of the elements of school improvement come together in practice. It begins from two assumptions. The first is that *all students have a potential for learning* that is not fully exploited (line 1). The second is that is that the students' learning capability refers to their ability to access that potential through *increasing their range of learning skills* (line 2). This potential is best realized and learning capability enhanced, through the range of *teaching and learning models* that the teacher uses with her/his students (line 3). It is the deliberate use of a range of teaching and learning strategies that are rich in metacognitive content that is one of the richest features of personalized learning. But, as has already been stressed, the teaching and learning strategies are not 'free floating', but *embedded in the schemes of work and curriculum content* that teachers use to structure the learning in their lessons (line 4). This leads to the whole school dimension through the staff development infrastructure the school has established, the *emphasis on high expectations*, the careful attention to consistency of teaching and the discussion of pedagogy that pervades the culture of the school (line 5). It is these forms of internal collaboration on personalized learning and 'professional' teaching that enable schools to *network* in order to raise standards across local areas, nationally and even globally (line 6).

Finally, while it is true that 'system leadership' is a relatively new concept, it is one that is not only fit for purpose but also finds a resonance with the outstanding school leaders of the day. It is also not an academic or theoretical idea, but has developed out of the challenges that system reform is presenting us with and the thoughtful, pragmatic and morally purposeful responses being given by our leading principals and heads. Ultimately, the test of system leadership is this – is it having an impact where it matters? Can our school leaders answer the hard questions?

Michael Barber (2005) phrases them like this:

- Who are your key stakeholders in the local community? Do they understand your vision? Are they committed to it? How do you know?
- Have you established a core belief that every pupil (yes, *every* pupil) can achieve high standards? And then have you reorganized all the other variables (time, curriculum, teaching staff, and other resources) around the achievement of that goal? If not, why not?
- Is each pupil in your school working towards explicit, short- and medium-term targets in each subject?
- Does each teacher know how his/her impact in terms of results compares to every other teacher? Have you thought about whether governors or parents should have access to this data? And what do you do to make sure that teachers who perform below the top quartile are improving?
- How do you ensure that every young person has a good, trusting relationship with at least one significant adult in your school?
- What do you and your school do to contribute to the improvement of the system as a whole?

These are the types of question that the best system leaders test themselves against and are now comfortable with. When all our school leaders can do so, then surely we are well on our way to every school being a great school.

Federations – system leadership in action

Over the past few years a model of school improvement based around 'leading schools' has been developed in England. 'Leading schools' are increasingly being expected to make the greatest contribution to supporting low-achieving and underperforming schools. They are also seen as the natural leaders of 'education improvement partnerships', which will take collective responsibility for lifting the performance of all children in a geographical area. This is a clear and direct response to the challenge posed by the segmentation of the secondary school system and demonstrates the power of system leadership.

Just because a school or school leader happens to be high performing, is no guarantee that they can assist other schools through their improvement process. Our research on the impact of a federation arrangement between a leading school and low-attaining or failing schools is instructive about the conditions necessary to make such a partnership successful. There are two key factors – the characteristics of the lead school and the nature of the process they engage in with their partner school – that are briefly described below.

In terms of lead school characteristics, it is clear that the pool to be drawn from contains those schools with an outstanding record of achievement. In addition, the following attributes seem to be critical:

- longevity of successful headship on the part of the lead school and a head, who sees their success in the success of others and, crucially, who understands the process of school improvement
- a tradition of teamworking among senior managers in both strategic and operational fields
- a middle management capacity in the lead school with skills of use of data, exam requirements, curriculum planning, pedagogy and mentoring
- a 'can do' attitude and energy on the part of those in the lead school that is infectious within their school and to those they are partnering
- these attributes need to be combined with a clearly defined process that systematically goes through a preparatory, development and exit phase. Although such a medium-term plan needs to be articulated on the part of the lead school, the partner school needs to feel, from the very beginning, that there is immediate and simultaneous action on the four key levers of improvement (viz. behaviour, management, curriculum, and teaching and learning). Through quick wins within a thought-through longer term strategy, the lead school begins to restore the confidence of all, including parents, and starts to build a culture of success. The key features of this are:
  - confronting the partner school with the realities of their situation
  - a subsequent practical action plan with a sense of urgency and pace that goes to the heart of the root causes and has the sharpest possible focus on raising test and examination results
  - a commitment to invade and saturate the partner school, especially in the early days, with the best of staff from the lead

school, and to use this as a basis for professionalizing the staff of the partner
- this 'invasion' uses the very best of transferable practices that have a proven track record in the lead school
- building capacity by matching staff and mentoring in the realization that quick wins are just that and sustainability must also be built
- planning for appropriate exit.

There is now growing evidence in the English secondary school system that this approach to system leadership is having a positive impact. Three examples make the point:

- Waverley School, under the leadership of Sir Dexter Hutt from Ninestiles, improved from 16% 5 A–Cs at GCSE in 2001 to 62% in 2004.
- Sir Michael Wilshaw has instilled excellent behaviour, a focus on teaching and learning, and high expectations at Mossbourne Academy, which is also having wider impact in the community.
- Valley Park School, under the leadership of Sue Glanville, improved from 31% 5A*–C in 2004 to 43% in 2005. The lead school, Invicta Grammar, also benefited by developing its leadership team and curriculum offer.

Although these results are very encouraging, this approach to school renewal is still very ad hoc, in England at least. In moving this strategy to scale, there are at least four key issues that have to be addressed, if system leadership is to have a system-wide impact. These issues emerged from our research on executive headship and recent seminars with system leaders.

The first is to do with *roles and responsibilities*, e.g. the need to balance clarity of roles with flexibility for professionals, and to see these roles as being distributed ones and not just about heads. Our respondents saw a wider pool of system leaders as a means to improve student success and address a declining supply of heads. Questioned whether roles should be clarified, they reported the following:

- desire to know who is doing what (i.e. the scope)
- a belief that clarity brings benefits: on models of practice and intelligent accountability
- lead schools need to demonstrate quality and 'readiness'

But, they were worried about restricting flexibility and suggested that these roles and responsibilities should:

- be professionally led
- be responsive to context
- be organic

The second relates to *agency and brokerage* in order to ensure that the whole approach is about schools supporting each other and not being 'done to', and to ensure that we move from the current ad hoc basis to large-scale well-organized activity. Our respondents agreed that a range of brokerage processes were needed to be contextually 'fit for purpose'. They reported that brokerage should:

- remain locally determined, as choosing the right partner is critical
- move to a larger scale, with LEAs required to seriously consider
- develop national infrastructure to support local partnerships

But they were concerned that tension remained between:

- local flexibility versus ad hoc inefficiency
- national support versus bureaucratization

The third is the importance of *tailored development*, to ensure an approach that is responsive to individual need, experience and context within a national framework to ensure standards and progression. Our respondents agreed that development should be responsive to need and context and promote a range of practices and not a single style. Questioned on 'tailored development' opportunities they suggested that they should be mainly informal, for instance:

- a toolkit of guidance and materials
- peer mentoring by existing system leaders

If it were to be more formalized, then:

- there was more enthusiasm for a national framework to ensure standards and progression, leading up to national education leader status than there was for a formal qualification

Finally, it was felt vital that issues of *accountability and funding* should be fully considered. So, for example, do the prevailing accountability frameworks sufficiently support system leadership? And is the funding available? Our respondent group was particularly concerned about provision of support and removal of disincentives. Questioned on how funding should be specified, they recommended that:

- partner schools pay to backfill in lead schools
- or should DfES lead funding, perhaps through a 'LiG-type' model?

They also suggested that accountability should be modified with:

- system leaders gaining specific powers to succeed in the face of resistance from (partner) school governors
- OFSTED inspections to include system leadership roles in criteria

Although this is only a brief description of a successful intervention strategy built on the federations' experience, it is clear how this can be adapted to suit support arrangements for all of schools, lead or partner, at whatever their stage in the performance cycle. It is in these ways that diversity and segmentation is used to transform the capacity of the school system.

Coda: towards a model of system leadership

We have seen glimpses in this chapter of a new educational landscape that is becoming better defined through a more systematic approach to segmentation and the power of system leadership. As the system leadership movement develops, we will find a new model of leadership flowing inductively from the actions of our best educational leaders. I have made an initial attempt to capture the main elements of this emerging practice in Figure 7.7. As such, it obviously builds on the logic of the discussion on system leadership in this chapter. What is distinctive about the model, is that the individual elements build on each other to present a theory of action for leadership in the new educational context.

The model exhibits a logic that flows from the inside out. Here, leaders, driven by a moral purpose related to the enhancement of student learning, seek to empower teachers and others to make schools a critical force for improving communities. It is premised on the argument made in this book, that sustainable educational development requires educational leaders who are willing to shoulder broader leadership roles: who care about and work for the success of other schools as well as their own.

Let me briefly unpack the elements in the model. It begins in the centre with the acknowledgement that such forms of leadership are imbued with moral purpose in the way in which we defined it earlier. Without that, there would not be the passion to proceed or the encouragement for others to follow. This, however, is necessary, but not in itself sufficient. Although I am not a great believer in attributional or heroic theories of leadership, it is clear from the practice of our best system leaders that there is a characteristic set of behaviours and skills that they share. As illustrated in the next ring of the

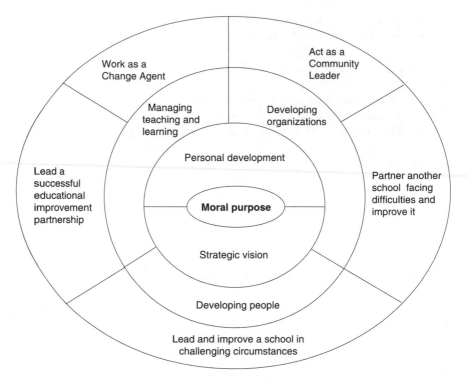

Figure 7.7   An emerging model of system leadership

diagram these are of two types. First, system leaders engage in 'personal development', usually informally through benchmarking themselves against their peers and developing their skill based in response to the context they find themselves working in. Second, all the system leaders we have studied have a strategic capability, and are able to translate their vision or moral purpose into operational principles that have tangible outcomes.

As denoted in the third ring of the model, the moral purpose, personal qualities and strategic capacity of the system leader find focus on three domains of the school – managing the teaching and learning process, developing people and developing the organization. These three aspects of system leadership have, as we have seen, a strong empirical base and are discussed in detail elsewhere in the book. To summarize very briefly, system leaders engage deeply with the organization of teaching, learning, curriculum and assessment in order to personalize learning for all their students, reduce within-school variation and support curriculum choice. In order to do this, they develop their schools as personal and professional learning communities, with relationships built across and beyond each school to provide a range of learning experiences and professional development opportunities.

Although there is a growing number of outstanding leaders who exemplify these qualities and determinations, they are not necessarily 'system leaders'. A system leader not only needs these aspirations and capabilities, but, in addition, as seen in the outer ring of the model, strives for equity and inclusion through acting on context and culture and through giving their communities a sense of worth and empowerment. They also, as we said earlier, realize that in order to change the larger system, they have to engage with it in a meaningful way.

So, in concluding, the purpose of this chapter has been to chart the emergence of a system leadership movement that can be increasingly clearly defined in terms of concepts, capacities, roles and strategy. What is exciting about the potential of such a movement, is that the practices of system leadership will grow out of the future demands of system leaders. Consequently, moving system leadership to scale, which is the forum of the final chapter, becomes an imperative.

8 Moving system leadership to scale

The narrative is almost complete. We began by using the metaphor of every school a great school as a means of capturing the essential purpose of a social democratic educational system with personalization at its heart. We used a number of case studies of large-scale reform, in particular England, to highlight the policy conundrum that a commitment to every school being great brings. The argument is not about either top-down or bottom-up change, but rebalancing them to create a networked system based on lateral accountability and learning. We discussed the four drivers that will assist us on that journey by continuing to raise standards and build capacity – personalized learning, professional teaching, intelligent accountability and networking and innovation. In the last chapter, we focused on diversity and segmentation as the means of building a new educational landscape and the role of school leaders in driving system reform.

But that is not the whole story. It is inevitable that in the process of rebalancing both the role of government and the role of schools will need to change. There has been much discussion in the previous chapters of how the work of teachers, school leaders and groups of schools will evolve and it would be easy to leave it at that. Easy, but fundamentally wrong. In discussions of this type many people, and not just the unreconstructed, see the distinction in oppositional rather than complementary terms. At any point in the figure we are now familiar with (reproduced here as Figure 8.1), the relationship between government and schools is reciprocal and its evolution dialectical. The critical point is that as the role of schools in the left-hand segment will be fundamentally different to their role in the right-hand segment, so will that of governments. The role of the government, both national and local, in the right-hand segment (shaded in the figure) will not be a pale imitation of that in the left segment, it will be different, more limited perhaps, but as crucial and potentially as vibrant.

The discussion would therefore be incomplete without exploring the role of government in the new educational landscape. In doing this, a good place to

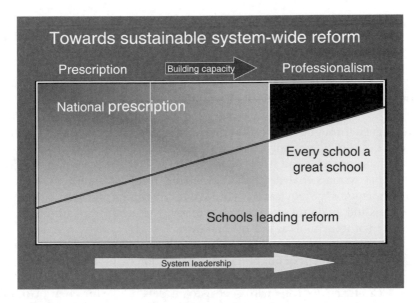

Figure 8.1 Towards sustainable system-wide reform

start is to return to the debate on the role of Third Way governments begun in the introduction and the initial chapters.

In *The Adaptive State* (2003: 27–9, 34) Tom Bentley and James Wilsdon argue that successful reform requires greater adaptive capacity at every level. They describe the adaptive state as follows:

> *If public services are going to achieve their full potential over the next generation, they must be reshaped through an open, evolutionary process. This process will not arise from the perpetual efforts to restructure existing arrangements, without changing the dominant assumptions governing models of organization. The opportunity now exists for systems that are flexible enough to personalize everything they offer, and responsive to the public they serve. To get the public services we deserve, 'modernization' must acquire a new meaning. In the long run, adaptability matters more than performance within rigid boundaries, so long as it can be shaped towards better life outcomes for everybody.*

Bearing this position in mind, I intend in this chapter to discuss how the 'adaptive state' can assist in moving system leadership to scale. In doing so I will briefly suggest some proposals for:

- moving system leadership to scale at the local level

- establishing a global movement for school reform
- finally, in the coda, a model for realizing the potential for system leadership.

Moving system leadership to scale

I have argued throughout that sustained large-scale improvements in learning outcomes cannot flow simply from government legislation. National prescription can take us so far, but it is when schools help to lead reform of national educational systems that deep and sustainable progress occurs. As we have seen, this requires 'system leaders' – heads who are willing and able to shoulder wider roles and, in doing so, to work to improve the success and attainment of students in other schools as well as their own.

At its heart, therefore, system leadership is about improving the deployment and development of our best leadership resources, in terms of:

- *Greater productivity*: with successful leaders deploying their own and their staff's knowledge and skills to improve other schools. Evidence from existing federations in England suggests that a national system of federations would be capable of delivering a sustainable step change in improvement in relatively short periods of time.
- *Spreading best educational practice*: system leaders are fundamentally committed to the improvement of teaching and learning. It is this mastery of the teaching and learning process that gives the system leader the licence and currency with which to engage with other schools and ensures the transfer of best practice around the system.

There is also a strong *social justice* potential through using our most capable leaders to help deliver a national system in which every child has the opportunity to achieve his/her full potential. This, however, raises two crucial issues:

1   Where does the agency come from to move these initiatives to scale?
2   How can this potential be deployed in areas of greatest disadvantage?

The traditional response has been intervention and management from government, national agencies or local authorities. The argument here is that this leadership now needs to come more from heads themselves or from agencies committed to working with them in authentic ways. It is clear that the more bureaucratic the response the less likely it will be to work. Is there a more lateral approach? Here are four interlinked suggestions and a proposal.

Suggestion 1: Incentivize rather than legislate

Create the conditions within the system to promote system leadership and such forms of collaborative activity through, for example, adjusting accountability requirements, and funding for capacity building. With the right incentives in place, schools will naturally move towards these new ways of working and mould them to the context in which they operate and to the challenges they face.

Suggestion 2: Place the agency close to the school

There are now in England for example, two emerging roles within the system – *national leaders of education* and *school improvement partners*, whose remit is school improvement. The intention that must be maintained is that instead of creating a new bureaucracy, their brief should increasingly focus on facilitating relationships between schools to maximize the potential of purposive collaboration. This approach to school transformation is made increasingly possible by the highly sophisticated data now available on school and student performance. These data enable groups of schools to identify (a) issues where they shared both strengths and weaknesses, i.e. their capacity for sharing and (b) common issues where they were likely to need some external input.

Suggestion 3: Use school independence collaboratively to tackle school failure in inner cities

The underlying assumption here is that, independent schools freed of local control, but working collaboratively, is a particularly appropriate organizational format for those schools, usually those in the inner cities, where rapid transformation of standards and support for students is most needed. The key point is that the freedoms associated with, say, trust status in England, can be used to promote collaboration and inclusion to directly address the needs of inner city students. The crucial condition is that the schools in the trust accept responsibility for the education of all the students within their geographic area. This arrangement will enable the now well-proven school improvement strategy, based on the best of practice in our most successful federations, to apply across a range of schools and to bring together a range of policy initiatives among them – extended schooling, personalized learning, 14–19 vocational reforms, high-performing schools – to give a real bite to the transformation of inner city schooling.

Suggestion 4: Develop system leadership as a movement

Currently, system leadership is regarded as an elite practice, but, if the aim is to improve learning by professionals working more closely across schools to lead reform, then system leadership must be turned into a national movement. In England again, for example, the Specialist Schools and Academies Trust (SSAT) is developing a multi-year programme of regional activity to initially develop the concept and skills of system leadership, with a focus on managing teaching and learning; and then to develop the application of system leadership in specific areas, with a focus on curricular specialism, tackling internal variation, delivering a wider 14–19 curriculum and extended schooling.

Education has already, however, through the uplifting of standards and skills, raised expectations in certain communities well beyond what was thought possible even a generation ago. These local successes now have to move to scale – hence the following proposal.

Proposal

Realizing this future, demands that we replace numerous national initiatives with a local consensus on a limited number of educational themes. Community renewal will thrive in circumstances in which, not only the local population is reinvigorated by raised aspirations and an improved environment, but also the providers themselves have their own sights raised by collaborative partnerships addressing the key priorities necessary for local transformation. Clearly, both must be fired by a shared vision and clarity of direction for the community concerned.

School partnerships and/or trusts offer the possibility of realizing such a future. In doing this, they should, therefore:

- Develop a vision of education that is shared and owned well beyond individual school gates. This implies networks of schools collaborating to build curriculum diversity, extended services, professional support and high expectations. The move towards networking should be developed and groups of secondary schools, in particular, should be encouraged to form collaborative arrangements outside local control.
- Seek to provide the majority of their CPD and innovative curricular practice from within, looking to external networks to enhance, enrich and deepen understanding as appropriate. In so doing, not only will they minimize cost and lost travel time, but they will also develop qualities, capabilities and expectations locally in ways which are certain to improve morale, self-confidence and credibility.
- Seek to share leadership and management expertise and innovation,

again looking periodically to external network providers for additional inspiration, guidance, challenge and support for impact.

- Use the full range of local expertise and resource (business management, mentoring and work-related opportunities, further and higher educational curriculum expertise and facilities as appropriate) and seek to maximize impact by bringing together resources targeted towards the same or similar outcome.
- Contribute substantially to the schools and regeneration agenda through coordination of such work and the related development of vocational pathways.
- Contribute substantially to the raising of families' aspirations and the safe and secure provision of children's services, such as extended school facilities and integrated provision, in order to make the local environment both safer and more engaged in transformation and renewal.

Collaboration can contribute decisively to a full range of government and local agendas by sharing of expertise, facilities and resources in educational specialism, innovation and creativity, leadership and management, vocational education and skills support. In addition, a full range of children's services agendas and constructive links between parents and schools, businesses and further higher education providers and schools are best served by such arrangements. The collective sharing of skills, expertise and experience creates much richer and more sustainable opportunities for rigorous transformation than can ever be provided by isolated institutions.

This strategic approach to educational transformation in local/urban areas is underpinned by an approach to system leadership that is reflected at three different levels:

- *System leadership at the school level* – with, in essence, school principals becoming almost as concerned about the success of other schools as they are about their own.
- *System leadership at the local/urban level* – with practical principles widely shared and used as a basis for local alignment (across an urban area) so that school diversity and collaboration are deliberately exploited with specific programmes developed for the most at risk groups.
- *System leadership at the national level* – with social justice, moral purpose and a commitment to the success of every learner providing the focus for transformation through, in this instance, advocacy for school trusts.

Although we have focused in this book on system leadership at the school level, the concept also applies, as we have just seen, at both national and local systems of government. Similarly, one could argue for a policy framework for system leadership at the international level, if we are to maximize the global diversity of educational systems. This issue is addressed briefly in the penultimate section of the book.

Global movements for school reform

Policy debates in many countries are often conducted with insufficient empirical evidence, and policy claims are often made on the basis of tradition, aspiration or ideology. What is needed is a policy framework that will allow countries to relate their policy choices more directly to student outcomes, to monitor the impact of changes in policy direction over time and possibly to compare policy options between countries. These are some of the issues I have been thinking through in a preliminary way with colleagues at the OECD responsible for the PISA programme.

Our initial analysis suggests that there now seem to be six 'policy drivers' that are being actively debated in many countries as being critical to not just enhancing student outcomes, but also to building capacity in the education system overall. This is not to say that these policy trends are accepted without controversy. In most countries, there are barriers to new policy trends that put implementation at risk. Barriers such as complacency, the opposition of teacher unions, overbureaucratization and policy incoherence among others all militate against the potential power of these trends to positively effect student performance. It must also be realized that these trends are often interpreted differently in different contexts and may well mean different things in different parts of a country. They do, however, provide the possibility of a framework in which to discuss global approaches to school change.

Three of these six policy drivers relate to teaching and learning and are consistent with the analysis conducted in this book:

- *Teaching quality.* Significant empirical evidence suggests that teaching quality is the most significant factor influencing student learning that is under the control of the school. The assumption is that teachers are on a par with other professions in terms of diagnosis, the application of evidence-based practices and professional pride. The image here is of teachers who use data to evaluate the learning needs of their students and are consistently expanding their repertoire of pedagogic strategies to personalize learning for all students. It also implies schools that adopt innovative approaches to timetabling and the deployment of increasingly differentiated staffing models.
- *Personalized learning.* As we have seen, the current focus on person-

alization is about putting students at the heart of the education process so as to tailor teaching to individual need, interest and aptitude in order to fulfil every young person's potential. A successful system of personalized learning means clear learning pathways through the education system and the motivation to become independent, e-literate, fulfilled, lifelong learners. Obviously, personalized learning demands both curriculum entitlement and choice that delivers a breadth of study and personal relevance.

- *School leadership and ethos.* The research based on school effectiveness has long identified the quality of leadership and the establishing of an ethos that is supportive of students as well as having high expectations as key factors. In terms of leadership, the core behaviours related to high standards are the ability of leaders to set a positive direction that links values to action, develops people – both staff and students – and develops the organization in order to reduce variation of performance within the school. Increasingly, these forms of leadership are distributed (i.e. not just the preserve of the head teacher) and systemic.

The three other policy drivers relate to the approaches to reform taken at the system level:

- *Standards and accountability.* There are two key purposes for accountability. The first is as a tool to support higher levels of student learning and achievement; the second is to maintain public confidence. In general, where there are high levels of student achievement and small variations of performance between schools then pressures from external accountability will be modest. Where there is a high degree of variability in school performance, then, it is likely that there will be calls for more robust forms of external accountability. In these situations the forms of accountability should always be designed to support teacher professionalism and the school's capacity to utilize data to enhance student performance.
- *Networking and collaboration.* This relates to the various ways in which networks of schools can stimulate and spread innovation as well as collaborate to provide curriculum diversity, extended services and community support. The prevalence of networking practice supports the contention that there is no contradiction between strong, independent schools and strong networks, rather than the reverse. Neither is there a contradiction between collaboration and competition – many sectors of the economy are demonstrating that the combination of competition and collaboration delivers the most rapid improvements.

- *Choice and contestability*. Real dynamism is being injected into the educational system of a number of countries by the judicious introduction of choice and contestability. Contrary to some popular beliefs, the introduction of choice under certain conditions will foster equity, in particular where choice for disadvantaged groups is combined with good information and additional funding. The introduction of new providers, i.e. contestability, and the strategic introduction of diversity are also proving to be a stimulus to innovation and the raising of standards in many jurisdictions. Within this broad policy area, there is also the opportunity for governments to target funding for those students most at risk of school failure. This incentive alone would do much to reduce inequity and stimulate choice and contestability.

As we have seen throughout the book, these policy drivers are equally important for individual schools or groups of schools as they are for national governments. What often happens, however, is that these trends tend to be worked on individually; rarely are the entire set of potential levers considered together at the same time. What is needed is a framework to help governments (and schools) to reflect on how best to balance these various strategies in a comprehensive approach to systemic educational change. Figure 8.2 (Barber 2005) provides an example of such a framework. It seeks to identify three key

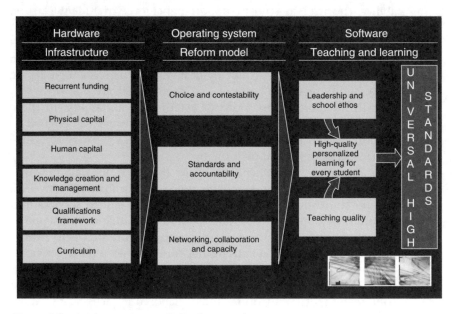

Figure 8.2　A coherent system design framework

elements of a coherent approach to school change. The framework also suggests how these three elements may interact and impact on the learning and achievement of students.

This educational model was developed by Michael Barber (2005) based on the Thomas Friedman analogy (in his book *The Lexus and the Olive Tree* (1999)) of a nation's economy being compared to a computer system. Originally developed for educational systems it can also apply to schools. There is the hardware – the infrastructure, funding and physical resources as well as human and intellectual capital. There is also the software – the interaction between the school and the student, the process of teaching and learning infused by the leadership of the school. In between the two, there is the operating system or the strategy for change the school or system chooses, or not, to employ to develop itself as a whole.

Many schools, as well as ministries of education, assume that there is a direct link between the hardware and the software – as long as the resources are in place then student learning will be satisfactory. This is rarely the case and the reason is simple. We need a change strategy to link inputs to outputs, because without it student and school outcomes will be unpredictable. With a clear strategy for change, such as that described in Chapter 6, schools will more likely be able to translate their resources more directly into better learning environments and therefore learning outcomes for their children.

The same argument goes for local and national governments. The existence of such a framework allows for a more intelligent debate over the policies adopted by different countries in terms of all three elements – the hardware, the software and the operating system and their *integrated impact* on standards of learning and achievement.

Coda: realizing the potential of system leadership

In many ways, the structure and argument of this book also reflect this framework. In the early chapters we discussed aspects of various national policies that provide the hardware or infrastructure for system improvement. The 'drivers', especially those related to the learning and teaching aspects, reflect the software aspects of the diagram. The concepts of system leadership, accountability and segmentation relate to the operating system.

We are now in a position to revisit the policy framework that underpinned the success of the first term New Labour educational reforms discussed in Chapter 2. The broad argument made there was that a national education strategy based on the principle of 'high challenge and high support' contained a complementary cocktail of policies that linked together:

- high standards with quality materials and professional development
- demanding targets but support for schools in the most challenging of circumstances
- accountability with increasing devolution of responsibility

– is highly effective at raising standards in the short term.

The 'high-support, high-challenge' strategy was an outstandingly successful operating system for the policy objectives of the first term New Labour government. But operating systems are not immutable; they evolve with their societies and changing educational demands. The subsequent argument in this book has been to stress that, for learning and achievement to continue to rise into the medium to long term, we need a different policy arrangement, because of the rebalancing of national prescription with schools leading reform. This rebalancing is necessary for building capacity for sustained improvement and leads to a transformed and re-imagined educational landscape implied by the right-hand segment of our ubiquitous rectangle.

The argument that has been building over the past six chapters is that, the policy framework for 'every school being great' is equally sophisticated in terms of its aspiration but is more reflective of a context that is radically different in terms of increasingly lateral responsibilities and alignments. This framework, which should be recognizable to those who have read so far, can be seen in Figure 8.3.

In the centre is system leadership with the implication noted earlier that it applies at a range of levels and roles within the system. The key policy drivers should also be familiar by now:

- The demand for personalization requires a professional practice for teaching.
- The systemic potential of networking and collaborations requires new arrangements for governance and agency.
- The realization of 'intelligent accountability' within the school needs to be matched by a willingness to fund students who are most 'at risk'.

For the sake of completeness, one can see that the 'every school a great school' policy framework is as appropriate for the right-hand segment of the rectangle as the original framework was to the left-hand segment in the early days of New Labour's educational reforms. This equilibrium is captured in Figure 8.4.

In concluding the argument of this book, it is important to remember that the challenge of 'system leadership' has great moral depth to it. It addresses directly the learning needs of our students, the professional growth of our

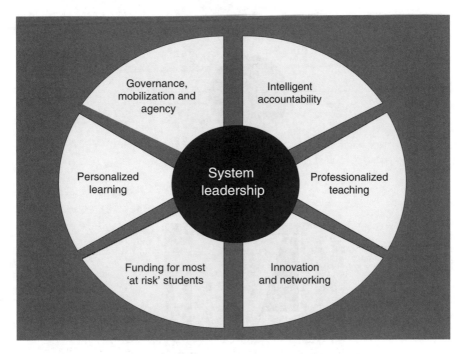

Figure 8.3 The 'every school a great school' policy framework

teachers and enhances the role of the school as an agent of social change. This is why I have argued at length that, as we imagine a new educational future in line with the 'policy conundrum' analysis outlined in Chapter 2, we require a new operating system capable of realizing a future where every school is a great one.

This is also, I suggest, in line with the earlier discussion of Etzioni and his vision of the 'good society'. Moral purpose in school reform is not just about raising levels of student achievement, as important as that is. It is also about empowering communities and contributing to a view of society that is inclusive and democratic. That is why this discussion on coherent system reform is so important. The operating system is not just a technical device for linking inputs to outputs; in the logic of this book, it is also a metaphor for those strategies that constitute a 'Third Way', that, when implemented, lead towards 'every school a great school' as well as the 'good society'.

Figure 8.4 Equilibrium contained in the 'every school a great school' policy framework

Bibliography

Adey, P.S. and Shayer, M. (1990) Accelerating the development of formal thinking in middle and high school students, *Journal of Research in Science Teaching*, 27(31): 267–85.

Adey, P. and Shayer, M. (1994) *Really Raising Standards. Cognitive Intervention and Academic Achievement*. London: Routledge.

Adey, P., Robertson, A. and Venville, G. (2001) *Let's Think!* Slough: NFERNelson.

Adey, P., Robertson, A. and Venville, G. (2002) 'Effects of a cognitive stimulation programme on Year 1 pupils', *British Journal of Educational Psychology*, 72(1): 1–25.

Adey, P., Nagy, F., Robertson, A., Serret, N. and Wadsworth, P. (2003) *Let's Think Through Science!* London: NFERNelson.

Assessment Reform Group (1999) *Assessment for Learning: Beyond the Black Box.* Cambridge: University of Cambridge Press, School of Education.

Assessment Reform Group (2002) *Assessment for Learning: Ten Principles.* www.qca.org.uk (accessed 19 May 2006).

Barber, M. (2001) Large-scale education reform in England: A work in progress. Paper prepared for the School Development Conference, Tartu University, Estonia.

Barber, M. (2004) The virtue of accountability. The inaugural Edwin J. Delattre Lecture, Boston University.

Barber, M. (2005) A 21st century self-evaluation framework. Annex 3 in Journeys of discovery: the search for success by design. Keynote speech in the National Center on Education and the Economy Annual Conference, Florida.

Becker, E. (1975) *Escape from Evil*. New York: Free Press.

Bennett, A. (2004) *A History of Boys: A Play*. London: Faber & Faber.

Bentley, T. and Wilsdon, J. (eds) (2003) *The Adaptive State*. London: Demos.

Bernstein, B. (1970) Education cannot compensate for society, *New Society*, 387(1): 344–7.

Black, P. and Wiliam, D. (1998) *Inside the Black Box: Raising Standards Through Classroom Assessment*. London: King's College.

Black, P., Harrison, C., Lee, C., Marshall, B. and Wiliam, D. (2002) *Working inside the Black Box: Assessment for Learning in the Classroom*. London: King's College, Department of Education and Professional Studies.

Blanchard, J. (2002) *Teaching and Targets. Self-Evaluation and School Improvement*. London: RoutledgeFalmer.

Bollen, R. and Hopkins, D. (1987) *School Based Review: Towards a Praxis*. Leuven: ACCO.

Brooks, G., Pugh, A.K. and Schagen, I. (1996) *Reading Performance at Nine*. Slough: NFER.

Brophy, J. (1983) Classroom organisation and management, *The Elementary School Journal*, 82(4): 266–85.

Brophy, J. and Good, T. (1986) Teacher behaviour and student achievement, in M. Wittrock (ed.) *Handbook of Research on Teaching*, 3rd edn. New York: Macmillan.

Bruner, J. (1960) *The Process of Education*. Cambridge, MA: Harvard University Press.

Bruner, J.S. (1966) *Towards a Theory of Instruction*. Cambridge, MA: Harvard University Press.

Cassell, A. and Kilshaw, D. (2004) *CAME Maths Project Department for Education and Skills*. www.standards.dfes.gov.uk (accessed 26 May 2006).

CERI (2005) *Formative Assessment. Improving Learning in Secondary Schools*. thesius. sourceoecd.org? (accessed 20 June 2006).

Chongde, L., Weiping, H., Philip, A. and Jilian, S. (2003) The influence of CASE on scientific creativity, *Research in Science Education*, 33(2): 143–62.

Collins, J. (2001) *Good to Great*. New York: HarperCollins.

Cordingley, P., Bell, M., Rundell, B. and Evans, D. (2003) *How Does Collaborative CPD for Teachers of the 5–16 Age Range affect Teaching and Learning? Evidence for Policy and Practice Information and Co-ordinating Centre (EPPI) with GTC, NUT and CUREE*. www.eppi.ioe.ac (accessed 18 May 2006).

Crandall, D., Eiseman, J. and Louis, K.S. (1986) Strategic planning issues that bear on the success of school improvement efforts, *Educational Administration Quarterly*, 22(2): 21–53.

Creemers, B.P.M. (1994) *The Effective Classroom*. London: Cassell.

Dalin, P. (1994) *How Schools Improve. An International Report*. London: Cassell.

Davies, B. (2005) Strategic leadership, in B. Davies, (ed.) *Essentials of School Leadership*. London: Paul Chapman.

DfEE/QCA (1999a) *Flexibility in the Secondary Curriculum*. London: DfEE/QCA.

DfEE/QCA (1999b) *The National Curriculum: Handbook for Primary Teachers in England*. London: HMSO.

DfEE (2001a) *Learning and Teaching: A Strategy for Professional Development*. London: Stationery Office.

DfES (2001b) *Schools Achieving Success*. London: Department for Education and Skills.

DfES (2002) *Investment for Reform*. London: Department for Education and Skills.

DfES (2003a) *Excellence and Enjoyment: A Strategy for Primary Schools*. London: Department for Education and Skills.

DfES (2003b) *Towards a Specialist System*. London: Department for Education and Skills.

DfES (2004a) *A National Conversation about Personalised Learning*. London: Department for Education and Skills.

DfES (2004b) *Excellence and Enjoyment: Learning and Teaching in the Primary Years*. London: Department for Education and Skills.

DfES (2004c) *Five-year Strategy for Children and Learners*. London: Department for Education and Skills.

DfES (2004d) *Improving Performance through Self-evaluation*. London: Department for Education and Skills.

DfES (2004e) *New Relationship with Schools: Improving Performance through Self-Evaluation*. London: Department for Education and Skills.

DfES (2005) *Higher Standards Better Schools for All*. London: Department for Education and Skills.

Earl, L., Katz, S., Elgie, S., Jaafar, S.B. and Foster, L. (2006) *How Networked Learning Communities Work*. Volume 1: *The Report*. Toronto: Aporia Consulting Ltd.

Earl, L., Watson, N., Levin, B., Leithwood, K., Fullan, M. and Torrance, N. with Jantzi, D., Mascall, B. and Volante, L. (2003) *Watching and Learning 3. Final Report of the External Evaluation of England's National Literacy and Numeracy Strategies*. Nottingham: Department for Education and Skills.

Edmonds, R. (1979) 'Effective schools for the urban poor', *Educational Leadership*, 39(1): 15–27.

Education and Skills Committee (2004) *Secondary Education: Schools Admission*. Fourth report of session 2003–04, Vol. II. London: The House of Commons.

Education and Skills Committee (2006) *The Schools White Paper: Higher Standards, Better Schools for All. First Report of Session 2005–06*, Vol. II. London: The House of Commons.

Elmore, R. (1995a) Getting to scale with good educational practice, *Harvard Educational Review*, 66(1): 1–26.

Elmore, R. (1995b) Teaching, learning and school organisation: principles of practice and the regularities of schooling, *Educational Administration Quarterly*, 31(3): 355–74.

Elmore, R.F. (2004) *School Reform from the Inside Out*. Cambridge, MA: Harvard University Press.

Etzioni, A. (2000) *The Third Way to a Good Society*. London: Demos.

Friedman, T. (1999) *The Lexus and the Olive Tree: Understanding Globalization*. New York: Anchor Books.

Fullan, M.G. (1999) *Change Forces: The Sequel*. London: Falmer Press.

Fullan, M. (2000) The return of large-scale reform, *Journal of Educational Change*, 1(1): 1–23.

Fullan, M. (2001) *The New Meaning of Educational Change*, 3rd edn. New York: Teachers' College Press.

Fullan, M. (2003) *The Moral Imperative of School Leadership*. London: Corwin Press.

Fullan, M. (2004) *Leadership and Sustainability. System Leaders in Action*. London: Sage.

Fullan, M. (2005) *Leadership and Sustainability*. London: Corwin Press.
Fullan, M. (2006) *Beyond Turnaround Leadership*. San Francisco: Jossey-Bass.
Fullan, M., Hill, P. and Creola, C. (2006) *Breakthrough*. London: Sage.
Gardner, H. (1993a) *Frames of Mind*, 2nd edn. London: Fontana Press.
Gardner, H. (1993b) *Multiple Intelligences: The Theory in Practice*. New York: Basic Books.
Giddens, A. (1998) *The Third Way: The Renewal of Social Democracy*. London: Polity Press.
Gladwell, M. (2000) *The Tipping Point: How Little Things Can Make a Big Difference*. London: Little, Brown.
Godin, S. (2001) *Unleashing the Ideavirus*. New York: Hyperion.
Gray, J., Hopkins, D., Reynolds, D., Wilcox, B., Farrell, S. and Jesson, D. (1999) *Improving Schools: Performance and Potential*. Buckingham: Open University Press.
Hargreaves, A. and Fink, D. (2006) *Sustainable Leadership*. San Francisco: Jossey-Bass.
Hargreaves, D.H. (2003a) *Educational Epidemic*. London: Demos.
Hargreaves, D.H. (2003b) *Working Laterally: How Innovation Networks Make an Education Epidemic*. London: DfES Publications.
Hargreaves, D.H. (2006) *Personalising Learning – 6*. www.specialistschools.org.uk (accessed 13 June 2006).
Hargreaves, D.H. and Hopkins, D. (1991) *The Empowered School: The Management and Practice of Development Planning*. London: Cassell.
Hargreaves, D.H., Hopkins, D., Leask, M., Connolly, J. and Robinson, P. (1989) *Planning for School Development*. London: Department of Education and Science.
Hautamäki, J., Kuusela, J. and Wikström, J. (2002, July) *CASE and CAME in Finland: 'The second wave'*. Paper presented at the 10th International Conference on Thinking, Harrogate.
Heifetz, R. (1994) *Leadership Without Easy Answers*. Cambridge, MA: Belknap Press.
Higham, R. and Hopkins, D. (2005) Report to the National College for School Leaders on School Federations.
Hopkins, D. (1987) *Knowledge Information Skills and the Curriculum*. London: The British Library.
Hopkins, D. (ed.) (1988) *Doing School-based Review*. Leuven: ACCO.
Hopkins, D. (2001) *School Improvement for Real*. London: RoutledgeFalmer.
Hopkins, D. (2002a) The Aga Khan Foundation School Improvement Initiative: An International Change Perspective in S.E. Anderson *Improving School through Teacher Development. Case Studies of the Aga Khan Foundation Projects in East Africa*. Rotterdam: Swets & Zeitlinger.
Hopkins, D. (2002b) *Improving the Quality of Education for All: A Handbook of Staff Development Activities*, 2nd edn. London: David Fulton.
Hopkins, D. (ed.) (forthcoming) *Innovative Approaches to Contemporary School Leadership*. London: OECD.

Hopkins, D and Higham, R. (forthcoming) Report to the National College for School Leaders on System Leadership.

Hopkins, D. and Levin, B. (2000) Government policy and school development, *School Leadership & Management*, 20(1): 15–30.

Hopkins, D., Reynolds, D. and Gray, J. (2005) *School Improvement – Lessons from Research*. Nottingham: DfES.

Hopkins, D., West, M. and Ainscow, M. (1996) *Improving the Quality of Education for All*. London: David Fulton.

Hopkins, D., Harris, A., Singleton, C. and Watts, R. (2000) *Creating the Conditions for Teaching and Learning. A Handbook of Staff Development Activities*. London: David Fulton.

Huberman, M. (1992) *Successful School Improvement. Reflections and Observations! A Critical Introduction to M. Fullan*. Milton Keynes: Open University Press.

Huberman, M. (1995) Networks that alter teaching: conceptualizations, exchanges and experiments, *Teachers and Teaching: Theory and Practice*, 1(2): 193–211.

Huberman, A.M. and Miles, M.B. (1984) Rethinking the quest for school improvement: some findings from the DESSI study, *Teachers' College Record*, 86(1): 34–54.

Hutchings, M., Smart, S., James, K. and Williams, K. (2006) *Survey on Teachers. GTC*. www.gtce.org.uk (accessed 26 August 2006).

Independent Schools Council (2006) *Independent Schools Educate*. www.isc.co.uk (accessed 2 June 2006).

Jackson, D. (2000) The school improvement journey: perspectives on leadership, *School Leadership and Management*, 20(1): 61–78.

Johnson, D.W., Johnson, R.T. and Holubec, J. (1993) *Cooperative Learning in the Classroom*, 6th edn. Edina, MN: Interaction Book Company.

Joyce, B.R. and Calhoun, E. (1998) *Learning to Teach Inductively*. Boston: Allyn Bacon.

Joyce, B.R. and Showers, B. (1995) *Student Achievement through Staff Development*, 2nd edn. New York: Longman.

Joyce, B.R. and Weil, M. (1996) *Models of Teaching*, 5th edn. Englewood Cliffs, NJ: Prentice Hall.

Joyce, B., Calhoun, E. and Hopkins, D. (1997) *Models of Teaching – Tools for Learning*. Buckingham: Open University Press.

Joyce, B.R., Calhoun, E.F. and Hopkins, D. (1999) *The New Structure of School Improvement*. Buckingham: Open University Press.

Joyce, B.R., Calhoun, E. and Hopkins, D. (2002) *Models of Learning – Tools for Teaching*, 2nd edn. Buckingham: Open University Press.

Kolb, D.A. (1984) *Experiential Learning*. Englewood Cliffs, NJ: Prentice Hall.

Leadbeater, C. (2004) *Learning about Personalisation: How can We put the Learner at the Heart of the Education System?* Nottingham: Department for Education and Skills.

Leithwood, K. Jantzi, D. and Mascall, B. (1999) Large-scale reform: what works?

Unpublished manuscript, Ontario Institute for Studies in Education, University of Toronto.

Leithwood, K., Day, C., Sammons, P., Harris, A. and Hopkins, D. (forthcoming) *Successful school leadership. What it is and how it influences pupil learning.* Report to the Department for Education and Skills.

Macbeath, J. (1999) *Schools Must Speak for Themselves: The Case for School Self-Evaluation.* London: Routledge.

Macbeath, J. and Sugimine, H. with Sutherland, G., Nishimura, M. and the students of the Learning School (2003) *Self-evaluation in the Global Classroom.* London: RoutledgeFalmer.

MacGilchrist, B., Mortimore, P., Savage, J. and Beresford, C. (1995) *Planning Matters.* London: Paul Chapman.

MacGilchrist, B., Myers, K. and Reed, J. (1997) *The Intelligent School.* London: Paul Chapman.

McLaughlin, M.W. (1990) The Rand Change Agent Study revisited: macro perspectives and micro realities, *Educational Researcher*, 19(9): 11–16.

Miliband, D. (2003) A modern social democratic education settlement. Speech, The Future of Comprehensive Secondary Education Seminar Series, Oxford University.

Miliband D (2004) Personalised learning: building a new relationship with schools. Speech by the Minister of State for School Standards to the North of England Education Conference, Belfast.

Morris, E. (2002) *Social Market Foundation Speech.* www.dfes.gov.uk/speeches (accessed 18 June 2006).

Mullis, I.V.S., Martin, M.O., Gonzalez, E.J. and Kennedy, A.M. (2003) *PIRLS 2001 International Report: IEAs Study of Reading Literacy Achievement in Primary School in 35 Countries.* Boston, MA: Boston College, International Study Center.

NASUWT (2005) *Initial Comment from Other Organisations on the Education White Paper Higher Standards – Better Schools for All.* www.teachers.org.uk (accessed 11 May 2006).

NCSL (2005) *Advice to the SoS on Complex Schools.* Nottingham: NCSL.

Newman, F., King, B. and Young, S.P. (2000) Professional development that addresses school capacity from urban elementary school. Paper presented to Annual Meeting of the American Educational Association.

OECD (2005) *The Definition and Selection of Key Competencies.* www.oecd.org (accessed 1 June 2006).

OECD/CERI (1999) *Innovating Schools.* hermia.sourceoecd.org/ (accessed 29 June 2006).

OFSTED (2004) *Standards and Quality 2002/2003 – The Annual Report of Her Majesty's Chief Inspector of Schools*, 4 February 2004 0–10–292677–8. London: Stationery Office.

OFSTED (2006) *Improving Performance Through School Self-evaluation and Improvement Planning. Further Guidance.* www.ofsted.gov.uk (accessed 27 June 2006).

O'Neill, O. (2002) A question of trust. The BBC Reith Lectures.

Osbourne, S.P. (ed.) (2000) *Public–Private Partnerships*. London: Routledge.

O'Shaughnessy, J. and Leslie, C. (2005) *More Good School Places*. London: Policy Exchange Limited.

PIRLS (2001) *PIRLS 2001 International Report: IEA's Study of Reading Literacy Achievement in Primary Schools*. Chestnut Hill: Boston College.

PISA (2000) *Knowledge and Skills for Life*. London: OECD.

PISA (2004) *Learning for Tomorrow's World*. London: OECD.

Renshaw, P. (1996) Commentary: adult–child interaction: can we move beyond traditional binaries? *Learning and Instruction*, 6(4): 399–404.

Rinehart, J. and Lindle, J.C. (1997) Pursuing a connection: does Kentucky's education reform reveal a relationship between student achievement and school level governance? Paper presented to the AERA, Chicago.

Rogoff, B. (1990) *Apprenticeship in Thinking. Cognitive Development in Social Context*. New York: Oxford University Press.

Rudduck, J. (1984) Introducing innovation to pupils, in D. Hopkins and M. Wideen, (eds) *Alternative Perspectives on School Improvement*. Lewes: Falmer Press.

Sebring, P., Bryk, A., Roderick, M., Camburn, E., Luppescu, S., Thum, Y.M., Smith, B. and Kahne, J. (1996) *Charting Reform in Chicago: The Students Speak*. Chicago: Consortium on Chicago School Research.

SHA (2003) *Towards Intelligent Accountability for Schools. A Policy Paper for School Accountability (Policy Paper 5)*. www.ascl.org.uk (accessed 24 June 2006).

SHA (2004) *Intelligent Accountability for Schools: One Year On. Progress Report on School Accountability by the Secondary Heads Association (Policy Paper 12)*. www.ascl.org.uk (accessed 13 May 2006).

Shayer, M. (1996) *The Long-term Effects of Cognitive Acceleration on Pupils' School Achievement*. London: King's College.

Shayer, M. (1999) Cognitive acceleration through science education II: its effect and scope, *International Journal of Science Education*, 21(8): 883–902.

Slavin, R.E. and Madden, N.A. (1999) *Disseminating Success for All: Lessons for Policy and Practice*. www.successforall.net (accessed 3 May 2006).

Slavin, R.E. and Madden, N.A. (2006) *Success for All/Roots and Wings. Summary on Achievement Outcomes Report 41*. www.successforall.net (accessed 15 May 2006).

Sockett, H. (1976) Teacher accountability, *Journal of Philosophy of Education*, 10(1): 34–57.

Stenhouse, L. (1975) *An Introduction to Curriculum and Development*. London: Heinemann Educational Books.

Stigler, J. and Hibbert, J. (1999) *The Teaching Gap*. New York: Free Press.

Stringfield, S., Ross, S.M. and Smith, L. (1996) *Bold Plans for School Restructuring*. New York: Lawrence Erlbaum.

Success for All Foundation (2006) *Summary of Research on the Success for All Reading Programs*. www.successforall.net (accessed 13 June 2006).

Teddlie, C. and Reynolds, D. (2000) *The International Handbook of School Effectiveness Research*. London: Falmer.

Vygotsky, L.S. (1962) *Thought and Language*. Cambridge, MA: MIT Press.

Webb, R. and Vulliamy, G. (2006) *Coming Full Circle? The Impact of New Labour's Education Policies on Primary School Teachers' Work*. www.atl.org.uk (accessed 27 June 2006).

Wenger, E. (1998) *Communities of Practice*. New York: Cambridge University Press.

Which (2005) *Which Choice?* Education: policy report.

Wood, D. (1998) *How Children Think and Learn: The Social Contexts of Cognitive Development*. Oxford: Blackwell.

Index

LEADERSHIP, GENDER AND CULTURE IN EDUCATION
MALE AND FEMALE PERSPECTIVES

John Collard and Cecilia Reynolds (eds)

This edited collection contains chapters by some of the world's leading scholars on gender and educational leadership. The chapters draw on research on men and women leaders in elementary, secondary and postsecondary schools in Australia, Canada, New Zealand, Sweden, the United Kingdom and the United States.

The authors counter essentialist claims about leaders that are based on biological, psychological and/or sociological theories that stress gender difference. Similarities between men and women and differences within gender groups are highlighted in this book. There are numerous discussions that employ sophisticated understandings of gender relations and leadership discourses in today's globalized context. Early scholarship on gender and leadership is supplemented here with more nuanced theories and explanations of how gender, race and class, for example, operate in connected and changing ways to affect the leadership experiences of men and women who work in different educational settings.

Contents

Contributors

Sandra Acker, Marie Battiste, Jill Blackmore, Cryss Brunner, John Collard, Marian Court, Anna Davis, Karin Franzen, Margaret Grogan, Olof Johannson, James Koschoreck, Betty Merchant, Cecilia Reynolds.

256pp   0 335 21440 1 (Paperback)   0 335 21441 X (Hardback)